T0294514

FROM LEADERSHIP THEORY TO PRACTICE

A Game Plan for Success as a Leader

Robert Palestini

Rowman & Littlefield Education
Lanham • New York • Toronto • Plymouth, UK

Published in the United States of America
by Rowman & Littlefield Education
A Division of Rowman & Littlefield Publishers, Inc.
A wholly owned subsidiary of The Rowman & Littlefield Publishing Group, Inc.
4501 Forbes Boulevard, Suite 200, Lanham, Maryland 20706
www.rowmaneducation.com

Estover Road
Plymouth PL6 7PY
United Kingdom

British Library Cataloguing in Publication Information Available

Library of Congress Cataloging-in-Publication Data

Palestini, Robert H.
    From leadership theory to practice : a game plan for success as a leader /
Robert Palestini.
        p. cm.
    ISBN 978-1-60709-022-9 (cloth : alk. paper) — ISBN 978-1-60709-023-6
(pbk. : alk. paper) — ISBN 978-1-60709-024-3 (electronic)
    1. Leadership. 2. Football coaches—United States. I. Title.
    HD57.7.P3485 2004
    658.4'092—dc22   2009002590

∞ ™ The paper used in this publication meets the minimum requirements of
American National Standard for Information Sciences—Permanence of Paper
for Printed Library Materials, ANSI/NISO Z39.48-1992.
Manufactured in the United States of America.

To Judy, out of whose fertile mind
came the idea for this book

To Karen, Scott, Robbie, and Brendan,
whose presence in my life is reinvigorating

To Liz and Vi for willingly giving
much needed technical support

CONTENTS

FOREWORD

I have known Bob Palestini for over fifteen years as a graduate dean and professor at Saint Joseph's University, my alma mater, as well as a highly successful high school basketball coach in the ultracompetitive Philadelphia Catholic League. His expertise and research interest is educational leadership. His twelve books on leadership have been outstanding in their own way, but this endeavor relates his theories on leadership to daily coaching and makes for a very interesting and intriguing connection.

Having just been the subject of a major motion picture, *Invincible*, which depicts my life story and how coaches impacted me both personally and professionally, I can relate to Dr. Palestini's basic premise that the tenets of situational leadership theory and effective coaching go hand in hand, whether we are discussing business, educational, or social settings.

In this book, the second in a series, Dr. Palestini demonstrates how the use of situational leadership theory by ten successful football coaches has contributed to their effectiveness and how these same leadership principles can be appropriately applied to anyone's leadership behavior, be the individual a parent, a teacher, an administrator, or a CEO. Each of us in our daily lives is asked to assume a degree of leadership responsibility. Dr. Palestini gives us a road map to follow, with excellence being the result. His book has practical applications that will allow each of us to develop and improve our leadership capabilities.

—Vince Papale

PREFACE

This is a book about leadership. The conventional wisdom is that leaders are born, not made. I disagree! My experience and, more importantly, scholarly research indicate that leadership skills can be learned. Granted, some leaders will be superior to others because of genetics, but the basic leadership skills are learned behaviors and can be cultivated and enhanced. The first chapter of this book speaks to the so-called science of administration, while the second chapter deals with the art of administration and leadership. One needs to lead with both mind (science) and heart (art) to be truly effective.

The effective building blocks of quality leadership are the skills of communication, motivation, organizational development, management, and creativity. Mastering the theory and practice in these areas of study will produce high-quality leadership ability and, in turn, produce successful leaders; doing so with "heart" will result in highly successful—what some authors have called heroic—leadership.

I would also dispute another broadly held assumption about effective leadership and administration—namely, that nice guys (and gals) finish last. To be a successful administrator, the belief goes, one needs to be firm, direct, even autocratic. Once again, scholarly research indicates, as does my own experience, that no one singular leadership style is consistently effective in all situations and at all times. Empirical and experiential studies indicate that effective leaders vary their styles depending on the situation. This *situational* approach is the underlying theme of this book. In the concluding chapter, I argue that truly effective leaders use both their minds and their hearts in the leadership process, and in doing so, nice guys and gals do oftentimes finish first.

Some thirty years ago, when I was coaching high school basketball, I attended a coaching clinic at which the main clinicians were Dean Smith, coach of North Carolina University, and Bobby Knight, then coach of Indiana University. Both coaches were successful then, and three decades later, they remain successful and, in one case at least, revered.

In the morning session, Bobby Knight explained how *fear* is the most effective motivator in sports. If you want athletes to listen to you, and you want to be successful, you need to instill fear in them, Knight stated. In the afternoon session, Dean Smith explained how *love* is the most effective motivator in sports. If you want to win and be successful, you must engender love in the athletes.

You can understand my sense of confusion by the end of that clinic. Here were two of the most successful men in sports giving contradictory advice. As a young and impressionable coach, these apparently mixed messages puzzled me. Over the intervening years, I have often thought about that clinic and tried to make sense of what I heard. After these many years, I have drawn two conclusions from this incident, both of which have had a significant impact on my philosophy of leadership and on this book.

The first conclusion has to do with the situational nature of leadership. Knight and Smith impressed upon me the truism that there is no one singular leadership style that is effective at all times and in all situations. The second is that, despite the possible short-term success of fear-based leadership, the better style for ensuring long-term success is one that inspires love, trust, and respect. Just as athletes become robotic and apprehensive about making mistakes when fear is the only motivator, so do employees who are supervised by an autocratic manager. Initiative, creativity, and self-sufficiency are all stymied by the leader who instills fear in his or her subordinates. Thus, I arrived at my conclusion that effective school administration and leadership, which is my field, and leadership in general begin with love, trust, and respect.

In addition to an emphasis on the nature of leadership, this book focuses on placing *theory* into practice. We cannot underestimate the value and importance of theory. Without theory, we have no valid way of analyzing and correcting failed practice. Without a theoretical base, we oftentimes lead by trial and error, or by the proverbial "seat of our pants." On the other hand, knowledge of theory without the ability to place it into reflective practice is neither of value nor characteristic of effective leadership. I suggest that leaders and aspiring leaders adopt one of the leadership theories described in this book and place it into reflective practice, modeled after the leadership behavior of some of the coaches highlighted here.

This book uses the case study approach in order to facilitate placing theory into effective practice. Each chapter contains an extensive study of one of ten of the most successful football coaches of our times. We will analyze each case and see how these coaches were able to place leadership theory into effective practice. I believe that the lessons learned will prove invaluable to leaders and aspiring leaders, be they parents, teachers, school principals, or CEOs.

I chose football coaches as my subjects because they are basically teachers, and as we shall see, the ability to teach one's followers, thus fostering a learning organization, is a valuable asset if one wishes to be an effective leader. I also chose coaches over other leaders because their leadership behavior is more observable and more chronicled.

This book also takes an organizational development approach to producing effective leadership. Picture yourself standing in the middle of a dense forest. Suppose you were asked to describe the characteristics of the forest: What types of trees are growing in the forest; how many acres of trees are there; where are the trees thriving; where are they not? Faced with this proposition, most people would not know where to start and would not be able to see the proverbial forest for the trees.

Newly appointed executives and administrators often have this same feeling of confusion when faced with the prospect of assuming a leadership role in a complex organization like a school or a company. Where does one start? An effective way to start would be to systematically examine the components that make up an organization. Such a system of organizational diagnosis and prescription will lead to a comprehensive and integrated analysis of the organization's strengths and weaknesses and point the way toward possible improvement. Using as a model the leadership implications found in the behaviors of the successful coaches profiled here, the final chapter of this book suggests such a sequential and systematic approach. Utilizing it effectively can produce dramatic and useful results.

This leads me to what I presumptuously refer to as my "Seven Principles of Effective Leadership." Effective leaders must

1. be able to adapt their *leadership style* to the situation;
2. be keenly aware of the organizational *structure and culture* of the institution;
3. be able to engender a sense of *trust and respect* in their followers;
4. continuously improve their organizations and, therefore, must be *agents for change*;
5. be *well organized* and *creative* and have a clearly articulated *vision*;
6. be able to *communicate* effectively and;
7. know how to *motivate* their followers and be able to *manage the conflicts* that arise.

In my view, which is supported by a prodigious amount of empirical research, if an administrator can master the knowledge and skills encompassed in these seven principles, and do it with heart, he or she will be highly successful.

I

CONTEMPORARY
LEADERSHIP THEORY

The effective functioning of social systems from the local PTA to the United States of America is assumed to be dependent on the quality of their leadership.

—Victor H. Vroom

INTRODUCTION

Leadership is offered as a solution for most of the problems of organizations everywhere. Schools will work, we are told, if principals provide strong instructional leadership. Around the world, administrators and managers say that their organizations would thrive if only senior management provided strategy, vision, and real leadership. Though the call for leadership is universal, there is much less clarity about what the term means.

Historically, researchers in this field have searched for the one best leadership style that will be most effective. Current thinking holds that there is no one best style. Rather, a combination of styles, depending on the situation the leader finds him- or herself in, has been deemed more appropriate. To understand the evolution of leadership theory thought, we will take a historical approach and trace the progress of leadership theory, beginning with the trait perspective of leadership and moving to the more current contingency theories of leadership.

THE TRAIT THEORY

Trait theory suggests that we can evaluate leadership and propose ways of leading effectively by considering whether an individual possesses certain personality, social, and physical traits. Popular in the 1940s and 1950s, trait theory attempted to predict which individuals successfully became leaders and then whether they were effective. Leaders differ from nonleaders in their drive, desire to lead, honesty and integrity, self-confidence, cognitive ability, and knowledge of the business they are in. Even the traits judged necessary for top-, middle-, and low-level management differed among leaders of different countries; for example, U.S. and British leaders valued resourcefulness; the Japanese, intuition; and the Dutch, imagination—but for lower and middle managers only.

The obvious question is, Can you think of any individuals who are effective leaders but lack one or more of these characteristics? Chances are that you can. Skills and the ability to implement the vision are necessary to transform traits into leadership behavior. Individual capability—a function of background, predispositions, preferences, cognitive complexity, and technical, human relations, and conceptual skills—also contributes.

The trait approach holds more historical than practical interest to managers and administrators, even though recent research has once again tied leadership effectiveness to leader traits. One study of senior management jobs suggests that effective leadership requires a broad knowledge of, and solid relations within, the industry and the company, as well as an excellent reputation, a strong track record, a keen mind, strong interpersonal skills, high integrity, high energy, and a strong drive to lead. In addition, some view the transformational perspective described later in this chapter as a natural evolution of the earlier trait perspective.

THE BEHAVIORAL PERSPECTIVE

The limited ability of traits to predict effective leadership caused researchers during the 1950s to view a person's behavior rather than that individual's personal traits as a way of increasing leadership effectiveness. This view also paved the way for later situational theories.

The types of leadership behaviors investigated typically fell into two categories: production oriented and employee oriented. Production-oriented leadership, also called *concern for production, initiating structure*, or *task-focused leadership*, involves acting primarily to get the task done. An administrator who tells his or her department chair, "Do everything you need to, to get the curriculum developed on time for the start of school, no matter what the personal consequences," demonstrates production-oriented leadership. So does an administrator who uses an autocratic style or fails to involve workers in any aspect of decision-making. Employee-oriented leadership, also called *concern for people* or *consideration*, focuses on supporting the individual workers in their activities and involving them in decision-making. A principal who demonstrates great concern for his or her teachers' satisfaction with their duties and commitment to their work has an employee-oriented leadership style.

Studies in leadership at Ohio State University, which classified individuals' styles as initiating structure or consideration, examined the link between style and grievance rate, performance, and turnover. Initiating structure reflects the degree to which the leader structures his or her own role and subordinates' roles toward accomplishing the group's goal through scheduling work, assigning employees to tasks, and maintaining standards of performance. Consideration refers to the degree to which the leader emphasizes individuals' needs through two-way communication, respect for subordinates' ideas, mutual trust between leader and subordinates, and consideration of subordinates' feelings. Although leaders can choose the style to fit the outcomes they desire, in fact, to achieve desirable outcomes in all three dimensions of performance, grievance rate, and turnover, the research suggested that managers should strive to demonstrate both initiating structure and consideration.

A series of leadership studies at the University of Michigan, which looked at managers with an employee orientation and a production orientation, yielded similar results. In these studies, which related differences in high-productivity and low-productivity work groups to differences in supervisors, highly productive supervisors spent more time planning departmental work and supervising their employees; they spent less time working alongside and performing the same tasks as subordinates, accorded their subordinates more freedom in specific task performance, and tended to be employee-oriented.

A thirty-year longitudinal research study in Japan examined performance and maintenance leadership behaviors. Performance here refers specifically to forming and reaching group goals through fast work speed; achieving outcomes of high quality, accuracy, and quantity; and observing rules. Maintenance behaviors preserve the group's social stability by dealing with subordinates' feelings, reducing stress, providing comfort, and showing appreciation. The Japanese, according to this and other studies, prefer leadership high on both dimensions over performance-dominated behavior, except when work is done in short-term project groups, subordinates are prone to anxiety, or effective performance calls for very low effort.

MANAGERIAL ROLES THEORY

A study of CEOs by Henry Mintzberg suggested a different way of looking at leadership. He observed that managerial work encompasses ten roles: three that focus on interpersonal contact—(1) figurehead, (2) leader, (3) liaison; three that involve mainly information processing—(4) monitor, (5) disseminator, (6) spokesman; and four related to decision-making—(7) entrepreneur, (8) disturbance handler, (9) resource allocator, (10) negotiator. Note that almost all roles would include activities that could be construed as leadership—influencing others toward a particular goal. In addition, most of these roles can apply to nonmanagerial as well as managerial positions. The role approach resembles the behavioral and trait perspectives because all three call for specific types of behavior independent of the situation; however, the role approach is more compatible with the situation approach and has been shown to be more valid than either the behavioral or trait perspective.

Though not all managers will perform every role, some diversity of role performance must occur. Managers can diagnose their own and others' role performance and then offer strategies for altering it. The choice of roles will depend to some extent on the manager's specific job description and the situation in question. For example, the tasks of managing individual performance and instructing subordinates are less important for middle managers than for first-line supervisors, and they are less important for executives than for either lower level of manager.

EARLY SITUATIONAL THEORIES

Contingency, or situational, models differ from the earlier trait and behavioral models in asserting that no single way of leading works in all situations. Rather, appropriate behavior depends on the circumstances at a given time. Effective managers diagnose the situation, identify the leadership style that will be most effective, and then determine whether they can implement the required style. Early situational research suggested that subordinate, supervisor, and task considerations affect the appropriate leadership style in a given situation. The precise aspects of each dimension that influence the most effective leadership style vary.

THEORY X AND THEORY Y

One of the older situational theories, Douglas McGregor's Theory X/ Theory Y formulation, calls for a leadership style based on individuals' assumptions about other individuals, together with characteristics of the individual, the task, the organization, and the environment (McGregor, 1961). Although managers may have many styles, Theories X and Y have received the greatest attention. Theory X managers assume that people are lazy, extrinsically motivated, and incapable of self-discipline or self-control and that they want security and no responsibility in their jobs. Theory Y managers assume that people do not inherently dislike work, are intrinsically motivated, exert self-control, and seek responsibility. A Theory X manager, because of his or her limited view of the world, has only one leadership style available, that is, autocratic. A Theory Y manager has a wide range of styles in his or her repertoire.

How can an administrator use McGregor's theory for ensuring leadership effectiveness? What prescription would McGregor offer for improving the situation? If an administrator had Theory X assumptions, he would suggest that the administrator change them and would facilitate this change by sending the administrator to a management-development program. If a manager had Theory Y assumptions, McGregor would advise a diagnosis of the situation to ensure that the selected style matched the administrator's assumptions and action tendencies, as well as the internal and external influences on the situation.

FREDERICK FIEDLER'S THEORY

While McGregor's theory provided a transition from behavioral to situational theories, Frederick Fiedler (Fiedler, 1987) developed and tested the first leadership theory explicitly called a contingency, or situational, model. He argued that changing an individual's leadership style is quite difficult and that organizations should put individuals in situations that fit with their style. Fiedler's theory suggests that managers can choose between two styles: task oriented and relationship oriented. Then the nature of leader–member relations, task structure, and position power of the leader influences whether a task-oriented or a relationship-oriented leadership style is more likely to be effective. "Leader–member relations" refers to the extent to which the group trusts and respects the leader and will follow the leader's directions. "Task structure" describes the degree to which the task is clearly specified and defined or structured, as opposed to ambiguous or unstructured. "Position power" means the extent to which the leader has official power, that is, the potential or actual ability to influence others in a desired direction owing to the position he or she holds in the organization.

The style recommended as most effective for each combination of these three situational factors is based on the degree of control or influence the leader can exert in his or her leadership position, as shown in table 1.1. In general, high-control situations (I–III) call for task-oriented leadership because they allow the leader to take charge. Low-control situations (VII and VIII) also call for task-oriented leadership because they require, rather than allow, the leader to take charge. Moderate-control situations (IV–VII), in contrast, call for relationship-oriented leadership because the situations challenge leaders to get the cooperation of their subordinates. Despite extensive research to support the theory, critics have questioned the reliability of the measurement of leadership style and the range and appropriateness of the three situational components. This theory, however, is particularly applicable for those who believe that individuals are born with a certain management style rather than that a management style is learned or flexible.

CONTEMPORARY SITUATIONAL LEADERSHIP

Current research suggests that the effect of leader behaviors on performance is altered by such intervening variables as the effort of subordinates, their ability to perform their jobs, the clarity of their job responsibilities, the organization of the work, the cooperation and cohesiveness of the group, the sufficiency of resources and support provided to the group, and the coordination of work group activities with those of other subunits. Thus, leaders must respond to these and broader cultural differences in choosing an appropriate style. A leader-environment-follower interaction theory of leadership notes that effective leaders first analyze deficiencies in the follower's ability, motivation, role perception, and work environment that inhibit performance and then act to eliminate these deficiencies.

PATH-GOAL THEORY

According to path-goal theory, the leader attempts to influence subordinates' perceptions of goals and the path to achieve them. Leaders can then choose among four styles of leadership: directive, supportive, participative, and achievement oriented. In selecting a style, the leader acts to strengthen the expectancy, instrumentality, and valence of a situation, respectively, by providing better technology or training for the employees;

reinforcing desired behaviors with pay, praise, or promotion; and ensuring that the employees value the rewards they receive.

Choosing a style requires a quality diagnosis of the situation to decide what leadership behaviors would be most effective in attaining the desired outcomes. The appropriate leadership style is influenced first by subordinates' characteristics, particularly the subordinates' abilities and the likelihood that the leader's behavior will cause subordinates' satisfaction now or in the future; and second by the environment, including the subordinates' tasks, the formal authority system, the primary work group, and the organizational culture. According to this theory, the appropriate style for an administrator depends on his or her subordinates' skills, knowledge, and abilities, as well as their attitudes toward the administrator. It also depends on the nature of the activities, the lines of authority in the organization, the integrity of their work group, and the task technology involved. The most desirable leadership style helps the individual achieve satisfaction, meet personal needs, and accomplish goals, while complementing the subordinates' abilities and the characteristics of the situation.

Application of the path-goal theory, then, requires first an assessment of the situation, particularly its participants and environment, and second, a determination of the most congruent leadership style. Even though the research about path-goal theory has yielded mixed results, it can provide a leader with help in selecting an effective leadership style.

THE VROOM-YETTON MODEL

The Vroom-Yetton theory involves a procedure for determining the extent to which leaders should involve subordinates in the decision-making process (Vroom, 1988). The manager can choose one of five approaches that range from individual problem solving with available information to joint problem solving to delegation of problem-solving responsibility. Table 1.1 summarizes the possibilities.

Selection of the appropriate decision process involves assessing six factors: (1) the problem's quality requirement, (2) the location of information about the problem, (3) the structure of the problem, (4) the likely acceptance of the decision by those affected, (5) the commonality of organizational goals, and (6) the likely conflict regarding possible

Table 1.1. Decision-Making Processes

For Individual Problems	For Group Problems
AI You solve the problem or make the decision yourself, using information available to you at that time.	AI You solve the problem or make the decision yourself, using information available to you at the time.
AII You obtain any necessary information from the subordinate, then decide on the solution to the problem yourself. You may or may not tell the subordinate what the problem is, in getting the information from him. The role played by your subordinate in making the decision is clearly one of providing specific information that you request, rather than generating or evaluating alternative solutions.	AII You obtain any necessary information from subordinates, then decide on the solution to the problem yourself. You may or may not tell subordinates what the problem is, in getting the information from them. The role played by your subordinates in making the decision is clearly one of providing specific information that you request, rather than generating or evaluating solutions.
CI You share the problem with the relevant subordinate, getting his ideas and suggestions. Then, you make the decision. This decision may or may not reflect your subordinate's influence.	CI You share the problem with the relevant subordinates individually, getting their ideas and suggestions without bringing them together as a group. Then you make the decision. This decision may or may not reflect your subordinates' influence.
GI You share the problem with one of your subordinates, and together you analyze the problem and arrive at a mutually satisfactory solution in an atmosphere of free and open exchange of information and ideas. You both contribute to the resolution of the problem with the relative contribution of each being dependent on knowledge rather than formal authority.	CII You share the problem with your subordinates in a group meeting. In this meeting you obtain their ideas and suggestions. Then, you make the decision, which may or may not reflect your subordinates' influence.
DI You delegate the problem to one of your subordinates, providing him or her with any relevant information that you possess, but giving responsibility for solving the problem independently. Any solution that the person reaches will receive your support.	GII You share the problem with your subordinates as a group. Together you generate and evaluate alternatives and attempt to reach agreement (consensus) on a solution. Your role is much like that of chairman, coordinating the discussion, keeping it focused on the problem, and making sure that the crucial issues are discussed. You do not try to influence the group to adopt "your" solution and are willing to accept and implement any solution that has the support of the entire group.

problem solutions. Figure 1.1 illustrates the original normative model, expressed as a decision tree. To make a decision, the leader asks each question, A through H, corresponding to each box encountered, from left to right, unless questions may be skipped because the response to the previous question leads to a later one. For example, a no response

A. Is there a quality requirement such that one solution is likely to be more rational than another?
B. Do I have sufficient info to make a high quality decision?
C. Is the problem structured?
D. Is acceptance of decision by subordinates critical to effective implementation?
E. If I were to make the decision by myself, is it reasonably certain that it would be accepted by my subordinates?
F. Do subordinates share the organizational goals to be attained in solving this problem?
G. Is conflict among subordinates likely in preferred solutions? (This question is irrelevant to individual problems.)
H. Do subordinates have sufficient info to make a high quality decision?

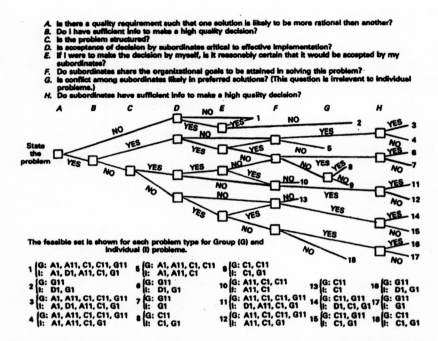

The feasible set is shown for each problem type for Group (G) and Individual (I) problems.

1 { G: A1, A11, C1, C11, G11 / I: A1, D1, A11, C1, G1 }
2 { G: G11 / I: D1, G1 }
3 { G: A1, A11, C1, C11, G11 / I: A1, D1, A11, C1, G1 }
4 { G: A1, A11, C1, C11, G11 / I: A1, A11, C1, G1 }
5 { G: A1, A11, C1, C11 / I: A1, A11, C1 }
6 { G: G11 / I: D1, G1 }
7 { G: G11 / I: G1 }
8 { G: C11 / I: C1, G1 }
9 { G: C1, C11 / I: C1, G1 }
10 { G: A11, C1, C11 / I: A11, C1 }
11 { G: A11, C1, C11, G11 / I: D1, A11, C1, G1 }
12 { G: A11, C1, C11, G11 / I: A11, C1, G1 }
13 { G: C11 / I: C1 }
14 { G: C11, G11 / I: D1, C1, G1 }
15 { G: C11, G11 / I: C1, G1 }
16 { G: G11 / I: D1, G1 }
17 { G: G11 / I: G1 }
18 { G: C11 / I: C1, G1 }

Figure 1.1.   Decision process flow chart for both individual and group problems.

to question A allows questions B and C to be skipped; a yes response to question B after a yes response to question A allows question C to be skipped. Reaching the end of one branch of the tree results in identification of a problem type (numbered 1 through 18) with an accompanying set of feasible decision processes. When the set of feasible processes for group problems includes more than one process (e.g., a no response to each question results in problem type 1, for which every decision style is feasible), final selection of the single approach can use either a minimum number of hours (group processes AI, AII, CI, CII, and GII are preferred in that order) as secondary criteria. A manager who wishes to make the decision in the shortest time possible, and for whom all processes are appropriate, will choose AI (solving the problem him- or herself using available information) over any other process. A manager who wishes to maximize subordinate involvement in the decision-making, as a training and development tool, for example, will choose DI or GII (delegating the problem to the subordinate or reaching a decision together with subordinates) if all processes are feasible and time is not limited. Similar choices can be made when analyzing individual problems. Research has shown that decisions made using processes from the feasible set result in more effective outcomes than those not included.

Suppose, for example, the teacher-evaluation instrument in your institution needed revising. Using the decision tree, we would ask the first question: Is there a quality requirement such that one solution is likely to be more rational than another? Our answer would have to be yes. Do I have sufficient information to make a high-quality decision? The answer is no. Is the problem structured? Yes. Is acceptance of the decision by subordinates critical to effective implementation? Yes. If I were to make the decision myself, is it reasonably certain that it would be accepted by my subordinates? No. Do subordinates share the organizational goals to be attained in solving this problem? Yes. Is conflict among subordinates likely in preferred solutions? Yes. Do subordinates have sufficient information to make a high-quality decision? Yes.

Following this procedure, the decision tree indicates that GII would be the proper approach to revising the teacher-evaluation form. GII indicates that the leader should share the problem with his or her faculty. Together they generate and evaluate alternatives and attempt to reach agreement on a solution. The leader's role is much like that of a chairperson coordinating the discussion, keeping it focused on the problem, and making sure that the critical issues are discussed. You do not try to influence the group to adopt "your" solution, and you are willing to accept and implement any solution that has the support of the entire faculty.

The recent reformulation of this model uses the same decision processes, AI, AII, CI, CII, GII, GI, DI, as the original model, as well as the criteria of decision quality, decision commitment, time, and subordinate development. It differs by expanding the range of possible responses to include probabilities rather than yes or no answers to each diagnostic question, and it uses a computer to process the data. Although both formulations of this model provide a set of diagnostic questions for analyzing a problem, they tend to oversimplify the process. Their narrow focus on the extent of subordinate involvement in decision-making also limits their usefulness.

THE HERSEY-BLANCHARD MODEL

In an attempt to integrate previous knowledge about leadership into a prescriptive model of leadership style, this theory cites the "readiness of followers," defined as their ability and willingness to accomplish a specific task, as the major contingency that influences appropriate leadership style. Follower readiness incorporates the follower's level of achievement motivation, ability and willingness to assume responsibility for his or her own behavior in accomplishing specific tasks, and education and experience relevant to the task. The model combines task and relationship behavior to yield four possible styles, as shown in figure 1.2. Leaders should use a *telling style*, provide specific instructions, and closely supervise performance when followers are unable and unwilling

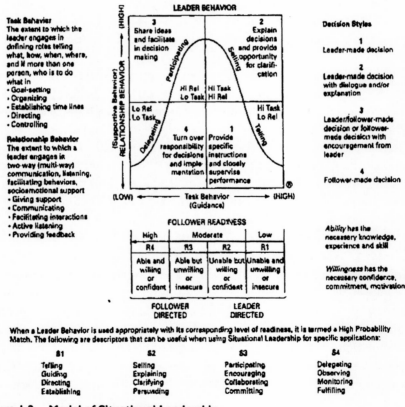

Figure 1.2.   Model of Situational Leadership

or insecure. Leaders should use a *selling style*, explain decisions, and provide opportunity for clarification when followers have moderate to low readiness. Leaders should use a *participating style*, where they share ideas and facilitate decision-making, when followers have moderate to high readiness. Finally, leaders should use a *delegating style*, giving responsibility for decisions and implementation to followers when followers are able, willing, and confident.

Although some researchers have questioned the conceptual clarity, validity, robustness, and utility of the model, as well as the instruments used to measure leadership style, others have supported the utility of the theory. For example, the Leadership Effectiveness and Description Scale and related instruments, developed to measure leadership style by life cycle researchers, are widely used in industrial training programs. This model can easily be adapted to educational administration and used analytically to understand leadership deficiencies, as well as combined with the path-goal model to prescribe the appropriate style for a variety of situations.

REFRAMING LEADERSHIP

Lee Bolman and Terrence Deal have developed a unique situational leadership theory that analyzes leadership behavior through four frames of reference: structural, human resource, political, and symbolic. Each of the frames offers a different perspective on what leadership is and how it operates in organizations (Bolman & Deal, 1991). Each can result in either effective or ineffective conceptions of leadership.

Structural leaders develop a new model of the relationship of structure, strategy, and environment for their organizations. They focus on implementation. The right answer helps only if it can be implemented. These leaders emphasize rationality, analysis, logic, fact, and data. They are likely to believe strongly in the importance of clear structure and well-developed management systems. A good leader is someone who thinks clearly, makes good decisions, has good analytic skills, and can design structures and systems that get the job done. Structural leaders sometimes fail because they miscalculate the difficulty of putting their designs in place. They often underestimate the resistance that it will generate, and they take few steps to build a base of support for their innovations. In short, they are often undone by human resource, political, and symbolic considerations. Structural leaders do continually experiment, evaluate, and adapt, but because they fail to consider the entire environment in which they are situated, they are sometimes ineffective.

Human resource leaders believe in people and communicate that belief. They are passionate about "productivity through people." They demonstrate this faith in their words and actions and often build it into a philosophy or credo that is central to their vision of their organizations. They believe in the importance of coaching, participation, motivation, teamwork, and good interpersonal relations. A good leader is a facilitator and participative manager who supports and empowers others. Human resource leaders are visible and accessible. Tom Peters and Robert Waterman popularized the notion of "management wandering around," the idea that managers need to get out of their offices and interact with workers and customers. Many educational administrators have adopted this aspect of management.

Effective human resource leaders empower; that is, they increase participation, provide support, share information, and move decision-making as far down the organization as possible. Human resource leaders often like to refer to their employees as "partners" or "colleagues." They want to make it clear that employees have a stake in the organization's success and a right to be involved in making decisions. When ineffective, however, they are seen as naive or as weaklings and wimps.

Political leaders believe that managers and leaders live in a world of conflict and scarce resources. The central task of management is to mobilize the resources needed to advocate and fight for the unit's or the organization's goals and objectives. They emphasize the importance of building a power base: allies, networks, and coalitions. A good leader is an advocate and negotiator, understands politics, and is comfortable with conflict. Political leaders clarify what they want and what they can get. Political leaders are realists above all. They never let what they want cloud their judgment about what is possible. They assess the distribution of power and interests. The political leader needs to think carefully about the players, their interests, and their power; in other words, he or she must map the political terrain. Political leaders ask questions such as, Whose support do I need? How do I go about getting it? Who are my opponents? How much power do they have? What can I do to reduce the opposition? Is the battle winnable? However, if ineffective, these leaders are perceived as untrustworthy and manipulative.

The symbolic frame provides still a fourth turn of the kaleidoscope of leadership. In this frame, the organization is seen as a stage, a theater in which every actor plays certain roles, and the symbolic leader attempts to communicate the right impressions to the right audiences. The main premise of this frame is that whenever reason and analysis fail to contain the dark forces of ambiguity, human beings erect symbols, myths, rituals, and ceremonies to bring order, meaning, and predictability out of chaos and confusion. Symbolic leaders believe that the essential role of management is to provide inspiration. They rely on personal charisma and a flair for drama to get people excited about, and committed to, the organizational mission. A good leader is a prophet and visionary, who uses symbols, tells stories, and frames experience in ways that give people hope and meaning. Transforming leaders are visionary leaders, and visionary leadership is invariably symbolic. Examination of symbolic leaders reveals that they follow a consistent set of practices and rules.

Transforming leaders use symbols to capture attention. When Diana Lam became principal of the Mackey Middle School in Boston, she knew that she faced a substantial challenge. Mackey had all the usual problems of urban public schools: decaying physical plant, lack of student discipline, racial tension, troubles with the teaching staff, low morale, and limited resources. The only good news was that the situation was so bad, almost any change would be an improvement. In such a situation, symbolic leaders will try to do something visible, even dramatic, to let people know that changes are on the way. During the summer before she assumed her duties, Lam wrote a letter to every teacher to set up an individual meeting. She traveled to meet teachers wherever they wanted, driving two hours in one case. She asked teachers how they felt about the school and what changes they wanted.

She also felt that something needed to be done about the school building because nobody likes to work in a dumpy place. She decided that the front door and some of the worst classrooms had to be painted. She had few illusions about getting the bureaucracy of the Boston public school system to provide painters, so she persuaded some of her family members to help her do the painting. When school opened, students and staff members immediately saw that things were going to be different, if only symbolically. Perhaps even more importantly, staff members received a subtle challenge to make a contribution themselves.

Each of the frames captures significant possibilities for leadership, but each is incomplete. In the early part of the twentieth century, leadership as a concept was rarely applied to management, and the implicit models of leadership were narrowly rational. In the 1960s and 1970s, human resource leadership became fashionable. The literature on organizational leadership stressed openness, sensitivity, and participation. In recent years, symbolic leadership has moved to center stage, and the literature now offers advice on how to become a visionary leader with the power to transform organizational cultures. Organizations do need vision, but this is not their only need, nor is it always their most important one. Leaders need to understand their own frame and its limits. Ideally, they will also learn to combine multiple frames into a more comprehensive and powerful style. It is this Bolman-Deal leadership theory on which I will base my conclusions regarding the leadership behavior of the ten football coaches profiled in this text.

TRANSFORMATIONAL LEADERSHIP

A charismatic, or transformational, leader uses charisma to inspire his or her followers and is an example of those who act primarily in the symbolic frame of leadership outlined above. He or she talks to the followers about how essential their performance is, how confident he or she is in the followers, how exceptional the followers are, and how he or she expects the group's performance to exceed expectations. Lee Iacocca and Jack Walsh in industry and the late Marcus Foster and Notre Dame's Rev. Theodore Hesburgh in education are examples of this type of leader. Virtually all of the coaches profiled in this study were found to be transformational leaders. Such leaders use dominance, self-confidence, a need for influence, and conviction of moral righteousness to increase their charisma and, consequently, their leadership effectiveness.

A transformational leader changes an organization by recognizing an opportunity and developing a vision, communicating that vision to organizational members, building trust in the vision, and achieving the vision by motivating organizational members. The leader helps subordinates recognize the need to revitalize the organization by developing a felt need for change, overcoming resistance to change, and avoiding quick-fix solutions to problems. Encouraging subordinates to act as devil's advocates with regard to the leader, building networks outside the organization, visiting other organizations, and changing management processes to reward progress against competition also help them recognize a need for revitalization. Individuals must disengage from, and disidentify with, the past, as well as view change as a way of dealing with their disenchantments with the past or the status quo. The transformational leader creates a new vision and mobilizes commitment to it by planning or educating others. He or she builds trust through demonstrating personal expertise, self-confidence, and personal integrity. The charismatic leader can also change the composition of the team, alter management processes, and help organizational members reframe the way they perceive an organizational situation. The charismatic leader must empower others to help achieve the vision. Finally, the transformational leader must institutionalize the change by replacing old technical, political, cultural, and social networks with new ones. For example, the leader can identify key individuals and groups, develop a plan for obtaining their commitment, and institute a monitoring system for following the changes. If an administrator wishes to make an innovative program acceptable to the faculty and the school community, for example, he or she should follow the above plan and identify influential individuals who would agree to champion the new program, develop a plan to gain support of others in the community through personal contact or other means, and develop a monitoring system to assess the progress of the effort.

A transformational leader motivates subordinates to achieve beyond their original expectations by increasing their awareness about the importance of designated outcomes and ways of attaining them; by getting workers to look beyond their self-interest to that of the team, the school, the school system, and the larger society; and by changing or expanding the individual's needs. Subordinates report that they work harder for such leaders. In addition, such leaders are judged higher in leadership potential by their subordinates as compared to the more common transactional leader.

One should be cognizant, however, of the negative side of charismatic leadership, which may exist if the leader overemphasizes devotion to him- or herself, makes personal needs paramount, or uses highly effective communication skills to mislead or manipulate others. Such leaders may be so driven to achieve a vision that they ignore the costly implications of their goals. The superintendent of schools who overexpands his or her jurisdiction in an effort to form an "empire," only to have the massive system turn into a bureaucratic nightmare, exemplifies a failed transformational leader. A business that expands too rapidly to satisfy its CEO's ego and, as a result, loses its quality control suffers the effects of transformational leadership gone sour. Nevertheless, recent research has verified the overall effectiveness of the transformational leadership style.

DEVELOPING A VISION

A requisite for transformational leadership is a vision. Although there seems to be a sense of mystery on the part of some individuals regarding what a vision is and how to create one, the process for developing one is not at all complex. Using education as an example, the first step is to develop a list of broad goals. "All Children Achieving" is an example of such a goal. These goals should be developed in conjunction with representatives of all segments of the school community; otherwise, there will be no sense of "ownership," the absence of which will preclude successful implementation.

The next step in the process is to merge and prioritize the goals and to summarize them in the form of a short and concise vision statement. The following is an example of a typical vision statement:

> Our vision for the Exeter School System is that all of our graduating students, regardless of ability, will say, "I have received an excellent education that has prepared me to be an informed citizen and leader in my community." Our students will have a worldview and, as a result of their experience in the Exeter School System, will be committed to a process of lifelong learning and the making of a better world by living the ideals of fairness and justice through service to others.

The key concepts in the above vision include all students achieving, excellence, leadership, multiculturalism, lifelong learning, values, and community service. It is these concepts that the transformational leader stresses in all forms of communication and in all interactions with the school community.

The final step in the process is the institutionalizing of the educational vision. This step ensures that the vision endures when leadership changes. Operationalizing and placing the important concepts of the vision into the official policies and procedures of the school system helps to institutionalize the educational vision and incorporate it into the school culture. As we will see, virtually all of the ten football coaches profiled in this book had a clear vision of what they wanted to achieve and convinced their teams to accept ownership of what would ultimately become their *shared* vision.

IMPLICATIONS FOR LEADERS

The implications of leadership theory for educational and other administrators are rather clear. The successful leader needs to have a sound grasp of leadership theory and the skills to implement it. The principles of situational and transformational leadership theory are guides to effective administrative behavior. The leadership behavior applied to an inexperienced faculty member may be significantly different from that applied to a more experienced and tested one. Task behavior may be appropriate in dealing with a new teacher, while relationship behavior may be more appropriate when dealing with a seasoned teacher.

The four frames of leadership discussed by Bolman and Deal (1991) may be particularly helpful to school leaders and leaders in general. Consideration of the structural, human relations, political, and symbolic implications of leadership behavior can keep an administrator attuned to the various dimensions affecting appropriate leadership behavior. With the need to deal with collective bargaining entities, school boards, and a variety of other power issues, the political frame considerations may be particularly helpful in understanding the complexity of relationships that exist between administrators and these groups. Asking oneself the questions posed earlier in relation to the political frame can be an effective guide to the appropriate leadership behavior in dealing with these groups.

SUMMARY

Recently, a plethora of research studies has been conducted on leadership and leadership styles. The evidence indicates overwhelmingly that no one singular leadership style is most appropriate in all situations. Rather, an administrator's leadership style should be adapted to the situation so that, at various times, task behavior or relationship behavior might be appropriate. At other times and in other situations, various degrees of both task and relationship behavior may be most effective.

The emergence of transformational leadership has seen leadership theory come full circle. Transformational leadership theory combines aspects of the early trait theory perspective with the more current situational, or contingency, models. The personal charisma of the leader, along with his or her ability to formulate an organizational vision and to communicate it to others, determines the transformational leader's effectiveness.

Since the effective leader is expected to adapt his or her leadership style to an ever-changing environment, administration becomes an even more complex and challenging task. However, a thorough knowledge of leadership theory can make some sense of the apparent chaos that the administrator faces on an almost daily basis.

Among scholars there is an assertion that *theory informs practice, and practice informs theory.* This notion posits that to be an effective leader, one must base his or her practice on some form of leadership theory. If the leader consciously based his or her practice on leadership theory, this would be an example of theory informing practice. On the other hand, when a leader utilizes theory-inspired behavior that is continually ineffective, perhaps the theory must be modified to account for this deficiency. In this case, practice would be informing or changing theory. This book examines the leadership behavior of ten successful football coaches to ascertain whether their behavior conforms to the principles of the Bolman-Deal situational leadership theory, and if it does not, to determine whether their practice needs to be modified or the theory needs to be modified to reflect effective practice. We also examine how these coaches' leadership practices can be applied to our own leadership behavior to make it more effective.

2

LEADING WITH HEART

Do unto others as you would have them do unto you.

—The Golden Rule

INTRODUCTION

How the leader utilizes the concepts contained in the preceding chapter depends largely on his or her philosophy of life regarding how human beings behave in the workplace. On one end of the continuum are those leaders who believe that human beings are basically lazy and will do the very least that they can to "get by" in the workplace. At the other extreme are those who believe that people are basically industrious and, if given the choice, would opt to do a quality job. I believe that today's most effective leaders hold the latter view. I agree with Max De Pree, owner and CEO of the highly successful Herman Miller Furniture Company, who writes in *Leadership Is an Art* that a leader's function is to "liberate people to do what is required of them in the most effective and humane way possible" (De Pree, 1989). Instead of catching people doing something wrong, our goal as enlightened leaders is to catch them doing something right. I would suggest, therefore, that in addition to a rational approach to leadership, a truly enlightened leader leads with heart.

Too often, leaders underestimate the skills and qualities of their followers. I remember Bill Faries, the chief custodian at a high school at which I was assistant principal in the mid-1970s. Bill's mother, with whom he had been extraordinarily close, passed away after a long illness. The school was a religiously affiliated one, and the school community went all out in its remembrance of Bill's mother. We held a religious service in which almost three thousand members of the school community participated. Bill, of course, was very grateful. As a token of his appreciation, he gave the school a six-by-eight-foot knitted quilt that he had personally sewn. From that point on, I did not know if Bill was a custodian who was a quilt weaver or a quilt weaver who was a custodian. The point is that it took the death of his mother for me and others to realize how truly talented our custodian was. So, our effectiveness as leaders begins with an understanding of the diversity of people's gifts, talents, and skills. When we think about the variety of gifts that people bring to organizations and institutions, we see that leading with heart lies in cultivating, liberating, and enabling those gifts.

LEADERSHIP DEFINED

The first responsibility of a leader is to define reality through a vision. The last is to say thank you. In between, the leader must become the servant of the servants. Being a leader means having the opportunity to make a meaningful difference in the lives of those who allow leaders to lead. This summarizes what I call leading with heart. In a nutshell, leaders don't inflict pain; they bear pain.

Whether one is a successful leader can be determined by looking at the followers. Are they reaching their potential? Are they learning? Are they able to change without bitterness? Are they able to achieve the institution's goals and objectives? Can they manage conflict among themselves? Where the answer to these questions is an emphatic yes, an effective leader resides.

I prefer to think about leadership in terms of what the gospel writer Luke calls the "one who serves." The leader owes something to the institution he or she leads. The leader is seen in this context as steward rather than owner or proprietor. Leading with heart requires the leader to think about his or her stewardship in terms of legacy, values, direction, and effectiveness.

LEGACY

Too many of today's leaders are interested only in immediate results that bolster their career goals. Long-range goals they leave to their successors. I believe that this approach fosters autocratic leadership, which oftentimes produces short-term results but militates against creativity and its long-term benefits. In effect, this approach is the antithesis of leading with heart.

On the contrary, leaders should build a long-lasting legacy of accomplishment that is institutionalized for posterity. They owe their institutions and their followers a healthy existence and the relationships and reputation that enable the continuity of that healthy existence. Leaders are also responsible for future leadership. They need to identify, develop, and nurture future leaders to carry on the legacy.

VALUES

Along with being responsible for providing future leaders, leaders owe the individuals in their institutions certain other legacies. Leaders need to be concerned with the institutional value system, which determines the principles and standards that guide the practices of those in the organization. Leaders need to model their value systems so that the individuals in the organization can learn to transmit these values to their colleagues and to future employees. In a civilized institution, we see good manners, respect for people, and an appreciation of the way in which we serve one another. A humane, sensitive, and thoughtful leader will transmit his or her value system through his or her daily behavior. This, I believe, is what Peter Senge refers to as a "learning organization" (Senge, 1990).

DIRECTION

Leaders are obliged to provide and maintain direction by developing a vision. I made the point earlier that effective leaders must leave their organizations with a legacy. Part of this legacy should be a sense of progress or momentum. An educational administrator, for instance, should imbue his or her institution with a sense of continuous progress, a sense of constant improvement. Improvement and momentum come from a clear vision of what the institution ought to be, from a well-planned strategy to achieve that vision, and from carefully developed and articulated directions and plans that allow everyone to participate in, and be personally accountable for, achieving those plans.

EFFECTIVENESS

Leaders are also responsible for generating effectiveness by being enablers. They need to enable others to reach their potential both personally and institutionally. I believe that the most effective way to enable one's colleagues is through participative decision-making. It begins with believing in the potential of people, in their diverse gifts. Leaders must realize that to maximize their own power and effectiveness, they need to empower others. Leaders are responsible for setting and attaining the goals of their organizations. Empowering or enabling others to help achieve those goals enhances the leader's chances of attaining them, ultimately enhancing the leader's effectiveness. Paradoxically, giving up power really amounts to gaining power.

EMPLOYEE OWNERS

We often hear managers suggest that a new program does not have a chance of succeeding unless the employees take "ownership" of the program. Most of us agree with the common sense of such an assertion. But how does a leader promote employee ownership? Let me suggest four steps as a beginning. I am certain that you can think of several more.

1. *Respect people.* As indicated earlier, this starts with appreciating the diverse gifts that individuals bring to your institution. The key is to dwell on the strengths of your coworkers rather than on their weaknesses. Try to turn their weaknesses into strengths. This does not mean that disciplinary action or even dismissal will never become necessary. It does mean that we should focus on the formative aspect of the employee-evaluation process before we engage in the summative part.

2. *Let belief guide policy and practice.* I spoke earlier of developing a culture of civility in your institution. If there is an environment of mutual respect and trust, I believe that the organization will flourish. Leaders need to let their belief or value system guide their behavior. Style is merely a consequence of what we believe and what is in our hearts.

3. *Recognize the need for covenants.* Contractual agreements cover such things as salary, fringe benefits, and working conditions. They are part of organizational life, and there is a legitimate need for them. But in today's organizations, especially educational institutions, where the best people working for these institutions are like volunteers, we need covenantal relationships. Our best workers may choose their employers. They usually choose the institution where they work based on reasons less tangible than salaries and fringe benefits. They do not need contracts; they need covenants. Covenantal relationships enable educational institutions to be civil, hospitable, and understanding of individuals' differences and unique charisms. They allow administrators to recognize that treating everyone equally is not necessarily treating everyone equitably and fairly.

4. *Understand that culture counts for more than structure.* An educational institution with which I have been associated recently went through a particularly traumatic time when the faculty and staff questioned the administration's credibility. Various organizational consultants were interviewed to facilitate a "healing" process. Most of the consultants spoke of making the necessary structural changes to create a culture of trust. We finally hired a consultant who believed that organizational structure has nothing to do with

trust. Instead, interpersonal relations based on mutual respect and an atmosphere of good will create a culture of trust. Would you rather work as part of a school with an outstanding reputation or work as part of a group of outstanding individuals? Many times these two characteristics go together, but if one had to make a choice, I believe that most people would opt to work with outstanding individuals.

IT STARTS WITH TRUST AND SENSITIVITY (HEART)

These are exciting times in education. Revolutionary steps are being taken to restructure schools and rethink the teaching–learning process. The concepts of empowerment, total quality management, using technology, and strategic planning are becoming the norm. However, while these activities have the potential to influence education in significantly positive ways, they must be based upon a strong foundation to achieve their full potential.

Achieving educational effectiveness is an incremental, sequential improvement process. This improvement process begins by building a sense of security within each individual so that he or she can be flexible in adapting to changes within education. Addressing only skills or techniques, such as communication, motivation, negotiation, or empowerment, is ineffective when individuals in an organization do not trust its systems, themselves, or each other. An institution's resources are wasted when invested only in training programs that assist administrators in mastering quick-fix techniques that, at best, attempt to manipulate and, at worst, reinforce mistrust.

The challenge is to transform relationships based on insecurity, adversariness, and politics into those based on mutual trust. Trust is the beginning of effectiveness and forms the foundation of a principle-centered learning environment that emphasizes strengths and devises innovative methods to minimize weaknesses. The transformation process requires an internal locus of control that emphasizes individual responsibility and accountability for change and promotes effectiveness.

TEAMWORK

For many of us, there exists a dichotomy between how we see ourselves as persons and how we see ourselves as workers. Perhaps the following words of a Zen Buddhist will be helpful:

> The master in the art of living makes little distinction between his work and his play, his labor and his leisure, his mind and his body, his education and his recreation, his love and his religion. He hardly knows which is which. He simply pursues his vision of excellence in whatever he does, leaving others to decide whether he is working or playing. To him he is always doing both.

Work can and should be productive, rewarding, enriching, fulfilling, and joyful. Work is one of our greatest privileges, and it is up to leaders to make certain that work is everything that it can and should be.

One way to think of work is to consider how a philosopher, rather than a businessman or -woman, would lead an organization. Plato's *Republic* speaks of the "philosopher-king," where the king would rule with the philosopher's ideals and values.

Paramount among the ideals that leaders need to recognize in leading an organization are the notions of teamwork and the value of each individual's contribution to the final product. The synergy an effective team produces is greater than the sum of its parts.

The foundation of the team is the recognition that each member needs every other member, and no individual can succeed without the cooperation of others. As a young boy, I was a very enthusiastic baseball fan. My favorite player was the Hall of Fame pitcher Robin Roberts of the Philadelphia Phillies. During the early 1950s, his fast ball dominated the National League. My uncle, who took me to my first ballgame, explained that opposing batters were so intimidated by Roberts's fastball that they were automatic "outs" even before they got to the plate. My uncle claimed that Robin Roberts was unstoppable. Even as a young boy, I intuitively knew that no one is unstoppable by himself. I said to my uncle that I knew how to stop Robin Roberts: "Make me his catcher."

EMPLOYEES AS VOLUNTEERS

Our institutions will not amount to anything without the people who make them what they are. And the individuals most influential in making institutions what they are, are essentially volunteers. Our very best employees can work anywhere they please. So, in a sense, they volunteer to work where they do. As leaders, we would do far better if we looked upon, and treated, our employees as volunteers. I made the point earlier that we should treat our employees as if we had a covenantal, rather than a contractual, relationship with them.

Alexander Solzhenitsyn, speaking to the 1978 graduating class of Harvard College, said this about legalistic relationships: "A society based on the letter of the law and never reaching any higher fails to take advantage of the full range of human possibilities. The letter of the law is too cold and formal to have a beneficial influence on society. Whenever the tissue of life is woven of legalistic relationships, this creates an atmosphere of spiritual mediocrity that paralyzes men's noblest impulses." And later, he continued, "After a certain level of the problem has been reached, legalistic thinking induces paralysis; it prevents one from seeing the scale and the meaning of events."

Covenantal relationships, on the other hand, induce freedom, not paralysis. As the noted psychiatrist William Glasser explains, "Coercion only produces mediocrity; love or a sense of belonging produces excellence" (Glasser, 1984). Our goal as leaders is to encourage a covenantal relationship of love, warmth, and personal chemistry among our employee volunteers. Shared ideals, shared goals, shared respect, a sense of integrity, a sense of quality, a sense of advocacy, a sense of caring: these are the basis of an organization's covenant with its employees.

THE VALUE OF HEROES

Leading with heart requires that an organization has its share of heroes, both present and past. We have often heard individuals in various organizations say, "So-and-so is an institution around here."

Heroes like these do more to establish an institution's organizational culture than any manual or policies-and-procedures handbook ever could. The senior faculty member recognized and respected for his or her knowledge, as well as his or her humane treatment of students, is a valuable asset to an educational institution. He or she symbolizes what the institution stands for. The presence of these heroes sustains the reputation of the institution and allows the workforce to feel good about itself and about the workplace. The deeds and accomplishments of these heroes need to be promulgated and to become part of the institution's folklore.

The deeds of these heroes are usually perpetuated by the "tribal story-tellers" in an organization. These are the individuals who know the history of the organization and relate it through stories of its former and present heroes. An effective leader encourages the tribal storytellers, knowing that they play an invaluable role in an organization. They work at the process of institutional renewal. They allow the institution to improve continuously. They preserve and revitalize the values of the institution. They mitigate the tendency of institutions, especially educational institutions, to become bureaucratic. These concerns are shared by everyone in the institution, but they are the special province of the tribal storyteller. Every institution has heroes and storytellers. It is the leader's job to see to it that things like manuals and handbooks don't replace them.

EMPLOYEE OWNERS

If an educational institution is to be successful, everyone in it needs to feel that he or she "owns the place." "This is not the school district's school; it is not the school board's school; it is my school." Taking ownership is a sign of one's love for an institution. In *Servant Leadership*, Robert Greenleaf writes, "Love is an undefinable term, and its manifestations are both subtle and infinite. It has only one absolute condition: unlimited liability!" Although it may run counter to our traditional notion of American capitalism, employees should be encouraged to act as if they own the place. It is a sign of love.

THE SIGNS OF HEARTLESSNESS

Up to now, we have dwelled on the characteristics of a healthy organization. In contrast, here are some of the signs that an organization is suffering from a lack of heart:

- There is a tendency to merely "go through the motions."
- A dark tension exists among key individuals.
- A cynical attitude prevails among employees.
- Finding time to celebrate accomplishments becomes impossible.
- Stories and storytellers disappear.
- There is the view that one person's gain must come at another's expense.
- Mutual trust and respect erode.
- Leaders accumulate, rather than distribute, power.
- Attainment of short-term goals becomes detrimental to the acquisition of long-term goals.
- Individuals abide by the letter of the law, but not its spirit.
- People treat students or customers as impositions.
- The accidents become more important than the substance.
- A loss of grace, style, and civility occurs.
- Leaders use coercion to motivate employees.
- Administrators dwell on individuals' weaknesses rather than their strengths.
- Individual turf is protected to the detriment of institutional goals.
- Diversity and individual charisma are not respected.
- Communication is only one-way.
- Employees feel exploited and manipulated.
- Arrogance spawns top-down decision-making.
- Leaders prefer to be served rather than to serve.

LEADERSHIP AS A MORAL SCIENCE

Here I address how educational administrators and other leaders should be educated and trained for their positions. Traditionally, there has been only one answer: practicing and future administrators should study educational administration in order to learn the scientific basis for decision-making and to understand the scientific research that underlies proper administration. Universities train future administrators with texts that stress the scientific research done on administrative behavior, review various studies of teacher and student performance, and provide a few techniques for accomplishing educational goals. Such approaches instill a reverence for the scientific method—as well as an unfortunate disregard for any humanistic and critical development of the art of administration.

I suggest a different approach. Although there is certainly an important place for scientific research in supporting empirical administrative behavior, I suggest that educational administrators also be *critical humanists*. Humanists appreciate the usual and unusual events of our lives and engage in an effort to develop, challenge, and liberate human souls. They are critical because they are educators and, therefore, are not satisfied with the status quo; rather, they hope to change individuals and institutions for the better and to improve social conditions for all. I will argue that an *administrative* science should be reconstructed as a *moral* science. An administrative science can be empirical, but it also must incorporate hermeneutic (the science of interpreting and understanding others) and critical dimensions. Social science has increasingly recognized that it must be informed by moral questions. The paradigm of natural science does not always apply when dealing with human issues. As a moral science, the science of administration is concerned with the resolution of moral dilemmas. A critical and literary model of administration helps to provide us with the necessary context and understanding wherein such dilemmas can be wisely resolved, and we can truly actualize our potentials as administrators and leaders.

One's proclivity to be a critical humanist oftentimes depends on one's philosophy of how human beings behave in the workplace. Worth repeating here are the two extremes of the continuum: those leaders who believe that human beings are basically lazy and will do the very least that they can to "get by" in the workplace and those who believe that people are basically industrious and, if given the choice, will opt to do the "right thing." I believe that today's most effective leaders hold the latter view. I agree with Max De Pree, owner and CEO of the highly successful Herman Miller Furniture Company, who writes in *Leadership Is an Art* that a leader's function is to "liberate people to do what is required of them in the most effective and humane way possible" (De Pree, 1989). Instead of catching people doing something *wrong*, our goal as enlightened leaders is to catch them doing something *right*. Such behavior is reflective of a leader who is in the humanist, if not also in the critical, tradition.

THE CRITICAL TRADITION

A *postpositivist leader* combines the *humanist* tradition with *critical* theory. Dissatisfaction with current administrative approaches for examining social life stems from administration's inability to deal with questions of value and morality and to fulfill its promise. For example, Griffiths (Griffiths & Ribbins, 1995) criticizes orthodox theories because they "ignore the presence of unions and fail to account for the scarcity of women and minorities in top administrative positions." David Erickson and Frederick Ellett ask, "Why has educational research had so few real implications for educational policy?" (Erickson, 1984). One answer is that an empiricist research program modeled on the natural sciences fails to address issues of understanding and interpretation. This failure precludes researchers from reaching a genuine understanding of the human condition. It is time, they argue, to treat educational research as a moral science. The science of administration can also be a moral one, a critically moral one.

The term *moral* is being used here in its cultural, professional, spiritual, and ethical sense, not in a religious sense. The moral side of administration has to do with the *dilemmas* that face us in education and other professions. All educators face three areas of dilemma: control, curricular, and societal. Control dilemmas involve the resolution of classroom management and control issues, particularly the issue of who is in charge and to what degree. Control dilemmas center around four questions: (1) Do you treat the child as a student, focusing narrowly on cognitive goals, or as a whole person, focusing more broadly on intellectual, aesthetic, social, and physical dimensions? (2) Who controls classroom time? In some classrooms, children are given latitude in scheduling their activities; in others, class activities follow a strict and mandatory schedule. (3) Who controls operations or the larger context of what it means to be human and how we resolve the inevitable conflicts that go on in the classroom? (4) Who controls the standards and defines success and failure?

Similar dilemmas occur in the curricular domain and relate to whether the curriculum is considered as received, public knowledge or as private, individualized knowledge of the type achieved through discoveries and experiments. These curricular difficulties also depend on whether one conceives of the child as customer or as an individual. The customer receives professional services generated from a body of knowledge, whereas the individual receives personal services generated from his or her particular needs and context.

A final set of dilemmas involves what children bring to school and how they are to be treated once there. One concerns the distribution of teacher resources. Should one focus more resources on the less talented, in order to bring them up to standards, or on the more talented, in order that they may reach their full potential? The same question arises in regard to the distribution of justice. Should classroom rules be applied uniformly, without regard to the differing circumstances of each child, or should family background, economic factors, and other sociological influences be considered? Should a teacher stress a common culture or ethnic differences and subcultural consciousness?

Much of teaching involves resolving such dilemmas by making a variety of decisions throughout the school day. Such decisions can be made, however, in a *reflective* or an *unreflective* manner. An unreflective manner means simply teaching as one was taught, without considering available alternatives. A reflective approach involves an examination of the widest array of alternatives. Thus, reflective teaching suggests that dilemmas need not be simply resolved but can be transformed so that a higher level of teaching expertise is reached.

This same logic can be applied to administration. Administration involves the resolution of various dilemmas, that is, the making of moral decisions. One set of dilemmas involves control. How much participation can teachers have in the administration of the school? How much participation can parents and students have? Who evaluates and for what purpose? Is the role of administration collegial or authority centered? The area of the curriculum brings up similar questions. Is the school oriented to basic skills, advanced skills, social skills, or all three? Should the curricula be teacher-made or national, state, or system mandated?

Should student evaluation be based on teacher assessment or standardized tests? What is authentic assessment? Finally, an additional set of dilemmas pertains to the idea of schooling in society. Should the schools be oriented to ameliorate the apparent deficits that some students bring with them, or should they see different cultures and groups as strengths? Should schools be seen as agents of change, oriented to the creation of a more just society, or as socializers that adapt the young to the current social structure?

Oftentimes, these questions are answered unreflectively and simply resolved on an "as needed" basis. This approach often resolves the dilemma but does not foster a real *transformation* in one's self, role, or institution. If administration and leadership encompass transformation, and I would argue that they should, then an additional lens to structural functionalism must be found through which to view these questions. I suggest that the additional lens be in the form of critical humanism and the Ignatian vision. In this context, then, administrative leadership can be viewed as a moral science.

THE IGNATIAN VISION

More than 450 years ago, Ignatius of Loyola, a young priest born to a Spanish aristocratic family, founded the Society of Jesus, the Jesuits, and wrote his seminal book, *The Spiritual Exercises*. In this book, he suggested a "way of life" and a "way of looking at things" that his religious community and other followers have propagated for almost five centuries. His principles have been utilized in a variety of ways. They have aided individuals in developing their own spiritual lives; they have been used to formulate a way of learning that has become the curriculum and instructional method employed in the sixty Jesuit high schools and twenty-eight Jesuit colleges and universities in the United States; and they have been used to develop individual administrative styles. Together, these principles comprise the *Ignatian vision*.

I wish to explore five Ignatian principles here as a foundation for developing an administrative philosophy and leadership style: (1) Ignatius's concept of the *magis*, or the "more"; (2) the implications of his notion of *cura personalis*, or "care of the person"; (3) the process of *inquiry* or *discernment*; (4) the development of *men and women for others*; and (5) service to the *underserved* and marginalized, or his concept of *social justice.*

At the core of the Ignatian vision is the concept of the *magis*, or the "more." Ignatius spent the greater part of his life seeking perfection in all areas of his personal, spiritual, and professional life. He was never satisfied with the status quo. He was constantly seeking to improve his own spiritual life, as well as his secular life, as leader of a growing religious community. He was an advocate of "continuous improvement" long before it became a corporate slogan, long before people like Edwards Deming used it to develop his Total Quality Management approach, and long before Japan used it to revolutionize its economy after World War II.

The idea of constantly seeking "the more" implies change. The *magis* is a movement away from the status quo, and moving away from the status quo defines change. The Ignatian vision requires individuals and institutions to embrace the process of change as a vehicle for personal and institutional improvement. For his followers, frontiers and boundaries are neither obstacles nor ends but new challenges to face, new opportunities to welcome. Thus, change needs to become a way of life. Ignatius further implores his followers to "be the change that you expect in others." In other words, we are called to model desired behavior—to live out our values, to be of ever fuller service to our communities, and to aspire to the more universal good. Ignatius had no patience with mediocrity. He constantly strove for the greater good.

The *magis* principle, then, can be described as the main norm in the selection and interpretation of information. Every real alternative for choice must be conducive to the advancement toward perfection. When some aspect of a particular alternative is *more* conducive to reaching perfection than other alternatives, we have reason to choose that alternative. Earlier, I spoke of the "dilemmas" that educators face during every working day. The *magis* principle is a "way of seeing" that can help us in selecting the better alternative.

At first hearing, the *magis* principle may sound rigid and frightening. It is absolute, and Ignatius is unyielding in applying it, but not rigid. On the one hand, he sees it as the expression of our love of humanity, which inexorably seeks to fill all of us with a desire not to be content

with what is less good for us. On the other hand, he sees that humanity has not only its particular gifts but also its limitations and different
stages of growth. A choice that in the abstract would be more humane
than it would be in the concrete would not be seen as adhering to the
magis principle. For example, tracking students according to ability can
be seen as humane in the abstract, but in the concrete, it can be dehu-
manizing. Ignatius would advise us to focus on the concrete in resolving
this dilemma.

In every case, then, accepting and living by the *magis* principle expresses our love of humanity. So, whatever the object for choice, the
measure of our love of neighbor will be the fundamental satisfaction
we will find in choosing and acting by the *magis* principle. Whatever
one chooses by this principle, no matter how undesirable in some other
respect, will always be what one would most want as a moral and ethical
member of the human race.

Closely related to the principle of the *magis* is the Ignatian principle
of *inquiry* and *discernment*. In his writings, he urges us to challenge the
status quo through the methods of inquiry and discernment. This is very
similar to one of the tenets of critical theory. In fact, the Ignatian vision
and critical theory share a number of norms.

To Ignatius, one must enter into inquiry and discernment to determine God's will. However, this process is of value for the purely secular
purpose of deciding which "horn of a dilemma" one should come down
on. To aid us in utilizing inquiry and discernment as useful tools in
challenging the status quo and determining the right choice, Ignatius
suggests that the ideal disposition for inquiry and discernment is humility. The disposition of humility is especially helpful when, despite one's
best efforts, the evidence that one alternative is more conducive to the
betterment of society is not compelling. When the discerner cannot find
evidence to show that one alternative is more conducive to the common
good, Ignatius calls for a judgment in favor of what more assimilates the
discerner's life to the life of poverty and humiliation. Thus, when the
greatest good cannot readily be determined, the *greater* good is more
easily discerned from the position of humility. These are very demanding standards, but they are consistent with the *magis* principle and the
tenets of critical humanism.

In addition to the *magis* principle norm, taking account of what has just been said and of what was said earlier about the norm of humility as a disposition for seeking the greater good, the relationship of the greater good norm to the greatest good norm can be clarified. The latter is absolute, overriding, and always primary. The greater good norm is secondary; it can never, in any choice, have equal weight with the first *magis* principle; it can never justify a choice of actual poverty and humiliation over riches and honors if the latter are seen to be more for the service of humanity in a particular situation of choice, with all its concrete circumstances, including the agent's responsibilities to others and his or her own stage of psychological and spiritual development. In other words, if being financially successful allows one to better serve the poor and underserved, that is preferred to actual poverty.

Ignatius presents us with several other supplemental norms for facing our "dilemmas." In choices that directly affect the individual person and the underserved or marginalized, especially the poor, Ignatius urges us to give preference to those in need. This brings us to his next guiding principle, *cura personalis*, or care of the person.

Another of Ignatius's important and enduring principles is his notion that, despite the primacy of the common good, the need to care for the individual person should never be lost. From the very beginning, the *cura personalis* principle has been included in the mission statement of virtually every high school and college founded by the Jesuits. It also impacts the method of instruction suggested for all Jesuit schools in the *ratio studiorum*, or "course of study," in these institutions. All Jesuit educational institutions are to foster what we now refer to as a "constructivist" classroom, where the student is an active participant in the learning process. This contrasts with the "transmission" method of instruction, where the teacher is paramount, and the student is a passive participant in the process. In the Ignatian vision, the care of the person is a requirement not only on a personal needs basis but also on a "whole person" basis, which would, of course, include classroom education.

This principle also has implications for how we conduct ourselves as educational administrators. Ignatius calls us to value the gifts and charisms of our colleagues and to address any deficiencies that they might have and turn them into strengths. For example, during the employee-evaluation process, Ignatius would urge us to focus of the formative stage of the evaluation far more than on the summative stage. This would be one small way of applying *cura personalis* theory to practice.

The fourth principle that I wish to consider is the Ignatian concept of service. Once again, this principle has been propagated from the very outset. The expressed goal of virtually every Jesuit institution is "to develop men and women for others." Jesuit institutions are called on to create a culture of service as one way of ensuring that their students, faculty, and staff reflect the educational, civic, and spiritual values of the Ignatian vision.

Institutions following the Ignatian tradition of service to others have done so through community-service programs and, more recently, service learning. Service to the community provides students with a means of helping others, a way to put their value systems into action, and a tangible way to assist local communities. Although these were valuable benefits, there was no formal integration of the service experience into the curriculum and no formal introspection concerning the impact of service on the individual. During the last ten years, there has been a movement toward creating a more intentional academic relationship. Service has evolved from a modest student activity into an exciting pedagogical opportunity. In the past, service was viewed as a cocurricular activity; today, it plays an integral role in the learning process.

Since many institutions are situated in an urban setting, service gives them a chance to share resources with surrounding communities and allows for reciprocal relationships to form between the university and local residents. Immersion in different cultures—economic, racial, educational, social, and religious—is the vehicle by which students make connections. Working side by side with people of varying backgrounds significantly impacts students, forcing them outside of their comfort zones and into the gritty reality of how others live. Through reflection, these students have the opportunity to integrate these powerful experiences into their lives, opening their eyes and hearts to the larger questions of social justice. Peter-Hans Kolvenbach, the former superior general of the Jesuit order, in his address on justice in American Jesuit universities in October 2000, used the words of Pope John Paul II to challenge Jesuit educators to "educate the whole person of solidarity for the real world" not only through concepts learned in the classroom but also through contact with real people.

Upon assuming the position of superior general in 1973 and echoing the words of Ignatius, Pedro Arrupe declared, "Our prime educational objective must be to form men and women for others; men and women who will live not for themselves but for others." In the spirit of these words, the service-learning movement has legitimized the educational benefit of all experiential activity. The term *service learning* means different things to different people, and debates on service learning have been around for decades, running the gamut from unstructured "programmatic opportunities" to structured "educational philosophies." At Ignatian institutions, service learning is a bridge that connects faculty, staff, and students with community partners and their agency needs. It connects academic and student life views about the educational value of experiential learning. It also connects students' textbooks to human reality and their minds and hearts to values and action. The programs are built on key components of service learning, including integration into the curriculum, a reciprocal relationship between the community agency and the student, and structured time for reflection, which is very much related to the Ignatian principle of *discernment* discussed earlier.

Participation in service by high school and college students, whether as a cocurricular or a course-based experience, correlates with where they are in their developmental process. Service work allows students to explore their skills and limitations, to discover what excites and energizes them, to put their values into action, to use their talents to benefit others, and to discover who they are and who they want to become. By encouraging students to reflect on their service, these institutions assist in this self-discovery. The reflection can take many forms: an informal chat, a facilitated group discussion, written dialogue, journal entries, reaction papers, or in-class presentations on research articles. By integrating the service experience through critical reflection, students develop knowledge about the communities in which they live and knowledge about the world that surrounds them. It is only after the unfolding of this service-based knowledge that the students are able to synthesize what they have learned with their lives. Through this reflection, the faculty members also have an opportunity to learn from and about their students. Teachers witness the change and growth of the students first hand. In short, service to others changes lives.

The implications of service to others for administration are clear. Not only can educational administrators enhance their effectiveness by including the idea of service to others in their curricula, but also by modeling it in their personal and professional lives. I have in mind here the concept of administrators becoming the "servant of the servants." Servant leaders do not inflict pain; they bear pain, and they treat their employees as "volunteers," a concept explored earlier.

Ignatius's concept of service leads into his notion of solidarity with the underserved (poor) and marginalized and his principle of social justice. We begin with an attempt to achieve some measure of clarity about the nature and role of social justice in the Ignatian vision. According to some, Ignatius defined justice in both a narrow and wide sense. The narrow sense involves "justice among men and women." In this case, it is a matter of "clear obligations" among "members of the human family." The application of this kind of justice would include the rendering not only of material goods but also of immaterial goods, such as "reputation, dignity, the possibility of exercising freedom."

Many of his followers also believe Ignatius defined justice in a *wider* sense, "where situations are encountered which are humanly intolerable and demand a remedy." Here, the situations may be products of "explicitly unjust acts" caused by "clearly identified people" who cannot be obliged to correct the injustices, although the dignity of the human person requires that justice be restored; or they may be caused by non-identifiable people. It is precisely within the structural forces of inequality in society that injustice of this second type is found, that injustice is "institutionalized," or built into economic, social, and political structures both national and international, and that people are suffering from poverty and hunger, from the unjust distribution of wealth, resources, and power. The critical theorists, of whom I spoke earlier, would likely concur with this wider definition of social justice.

It is almost certain that Ignatius did not only concern himself with purely economic injustices. He often cites injustices about "threats to human life and its quality," "racial and political discrimination," and loss of respect for the "rights of individuals or groups." When one adds to these the "vast range of injustices" enumerated in his writings, one sees that the Ignatian vision understands its mission of justice to include "the widest possible view of justice," involving every area where there is an attack on human rights. We can conclude, therefore, that although Ignatius was, to some degree, concerned about commutative justice (right relationships between private persons and groups) and distributive justice (the obligations of the state to render to the individual what is his or her due), he is most concerned about what, today, is generally called social justice, or "justice of the common good." Such justice is comprehensive and includes the above-mentioned strict legal rights and duties, but it is more concerned about the natural rights and duties of individuals, families, communities, and the community of nations toward one another as members of the common family of human beings. Every form of justice is included in, and presupposed by, social justice, but social justice emphasizes the social nature of the person, as well as the social significance of all earthly goods, the purpose of which is to aid all members of the human community to attain their dignity as human beings. Many of Ignatius's followers believe that this dignity is being undermined in our world today, and their main efforts are aimed toward restoring that dignity.

In the pursuit of social justice, Ignatius calls on his followers to be "in solidarity with the poor." The next logical question might then be, Who are the poor? The poor are usually thought to be those who are economically deprived and politically oppressed. Thus, we can conclude that promoting justice means working to overcome the oppressions or injustices that make the poor poor. The fallacy here, however, is that the poor are not necessarily oppressed or suffering injustice, and so Ignatius argues that our obligation toward the poor must be understood as linking "inhuman levels of poverty and injustice" and not as concerned with the "lot of those possessing only modest resources," even though those of modest means are often poor and oppressed. So, we conclude that the poor include those "wrongfully" impoverished or dispossessed.

An extended definition of the poor, one that Ignatius would espouse, would include any of the following types of people:

- First are those who are economically deprived and socially marginalized and oppressed, especially, but not limited to, those with whom one has immediate contact and is in a position to affect positively.
- The second group includes the "poor in spirit," that is, those who lack a value system or an ethical and moral sense.

- The third group includes those who are emotionally poor, who have psychological and emotional shortcomings and are in need of comfort.

In defining the poor in the broadest way, Ignatius exhorts us to undertake social change in our role as leaders, to do what we can do to bring an end to inequality, oppression, and injustice. Once again, we can see the close connection between the Ignatian principles of social justice and the main tenets of critical theory.

IMPLICATIONS FOR ADMINISTRATION

Each of the principles of the Ignatian vision noted above has a variety of implications for leaders. The *magis* principle has implications for administrators in that it calls for us to be seeking perfection continually in all that we do. In effect, this means that we must seek to improve continually. And since improvement implies change, we need to be champions of needed change in our institutions. This means that we have to model a tolerance for change and embrace not only our own change initiatives but also those in other parts of the organization.

The principle of *cura personalis* has additional implications. To practice the Ignatian vision, one must treat people with dignity under all circumstances. *Cura personalis* also requires us to extend ourselves in offering individual attention and attending to the needs of all those with whom we come into contact. Being sensitive to the individual's unique needs is particularly required. Many times in our efforts to treat people equally, we fail to treat them fairly and equitably. Certain individuals have greater needs than others, and many times these needs require that exceptions be made on their behalf. For example, if an adult student does not hand in an assignment on time, but the tardiness is due to the fact that he or she is going through some personal trauma at the moment, the principle of *cura personalis* calls on us to make an exception. Many would likely consider such an exception to be unfair to those who made the effort to complete the assignment in a timely manner; others might object that we cannot possibly be sensitive to the special needs of all of our students and colleagues. However, as long as the exception is made for anyone in the same circumstances, Ignatius would not perceive this exception as unfair. In fact, the exception would be expected if one is practicing the principle of "care of the person."

The Ignatian process of *discernment* requires educational administrators to be reflective practitioners. It calls on us to be introspective regarding our administrative and leadership behavior. We are asked to reflect on the ramifications of our decisions, especially in light of their cumulative effect on the equitable distribution of power and on the marginalized individuals and groups in our communities. In effect, the principle of discernment galvanizes the other principles embodied in the Ignatian vision. During the discernment process, we are asked to reflect upon how our planned behavior will manifest the *magis* principle, *cura personalis,* and service to the community, especially the underserved, marginalized, and oppressed.

The development of men and women for others requires that one have a sense of service toward those with whom the leader interacts and also develops this spirit of service in others. The concept of "servant leadership" requires us to encourage others toward a life and career of service and to assume the position of being the "servant of the servants." Ignatius thinks about leadership in terms of what the gospel writer Luke calls the "one who serves." The leader owes something to the institution he or she leads. The leader is seen in this context as steward rather than owner or proprietor.

The implications of Ignatius's notion of social justice are myriad for the administrator. Concern for the marginalized among our constituencies is required. We are called upon to be sensitive to those individuals and groups that do not share equitably in the distribution of power and influence. Participative decision-making and collaborative behavior is encouraged among administrators imbued with the Ignatian tradition. Equitable representation of all segments of the school community should be provided whenever feasible. Leadership behavior such as this will assure that the dominant culture is not perpetuated to the detriment of the minority culture, rendering the minorities powerless. We will find in the succeeding chapters that the most effective of the football coaches profiled incorporate many of the Ignatian concepts into their leadership behavior.

SUMMARY

I began this book by suggesting that leaders are made, not born. I posited that if one could master the skills involved in effective leadership, one could become a successful administrator. In this chapter, however, I assert that learning the skills involved in effective leadership is only part of the story. Leadership is as much an art, a belief, a condition of the heart, as it is the mastery of set of skills and an understanding of leadership theory. A truly successful leader, therefore, is one who leads with both the *mind* and the *heart*. When we look at the leadership behavior of the ten football coaches included in this study, we should consider not only whether their leadership practices conform to the Bolman-Deal situational leadership theory but also whether they are leading with *heart*. I believe we will find that those coaches who are most comfortable operating in Bolman and Deal's human resource frame of leadership are most likely to be leading with heart. At any rate, the most effective leaders will be those who lead with both mind (structural and political frames) and heart (human resource and symbolic frames).

❸

BILL BELICHICK

There is only one way to do anything: the right way.

—Golda Meir

BACKGROUND

Born in 1952, Bill Belichick is currently the head coach of the New England Patriots of the National Football League. Belichick got his first head coaching job with the Cleveland Browns in 1991 after spending his first fifteen seasons as an assistant coach. Of his five seasons coaching Cleveland, he had only one winning season. After being fired in 1995, he spent five years as an assistant coach before getting another head coaching opportunity in 2000 with the New England Patriots. Since then, Belichick has coached the Patriots to three Super Bowl victories and was named the Associated Press NFL Coach of the Year three times. In 2007 Belichick became the first coach in history to lead his team to a 16–0 regular season. However, the Patriot's dream of a perfect season was denied when they lost to the New York Giants in the Super Bowl.

Belichick was born in Nashville, Tennessee, but moved to Annapolis, Maryland, where his father, Steve, a former Detroit Lions player, was

an assistant football coach at the U.S. Naval Academy. After graduating
from high school, Belechick attended Wesleyan University in Middle-
town, Connecticut, where he played on the football team.

After graduating from Wesleyan, he took an assistant coaching position with the Baltimore Colts. In 1976, Belichick joined the Detroit
Lions as their assistant special teams coach and continued there until
1978. He then spent one year with the Denver Broncos as their assistant
special teams coach and defensive assistant. Next, Belichick began a
twelve-year stint with the New York Giants under head coach Ray Perkins. He was a defensive and special teams coach. He became the Giants' defensive coordinator in 1985 under head coach Bill Parcells, who
had replaced Perkins in 1983. His reputation as a defensive specialist
grew to the point where he was sought by virtually every team that had
an opening for a head coach. He received much credit for the Giants'
winning Super Bowls following the 1986 and 1990 seasons.

In 1991, he finally became a head coach with the Cleveland Browns.
During his tenure in Cleveland, he compiled a 36–44 record while lead-
ing the team to its most recent play-off-game win in 1994. However,
Belichick was fired after the 1995 season. After leaving Cleveland,
Belichick served under Parcells again as assistant head coach with the
New England Patriots for the 1996 season. The Patriots won the AFC
Championship that year, but lost to the Green Bay Packers in the Super
Bowl.

Belichick then moved with his mentor Parcells to the New York Jets.
When Parcells stepped down as head coach in 1999, Belichick became
the new Jets' head coach. However, Belichick no sooner accepted the
Jets' job before he announced his resignation. A few days later, he accepted an offer from the New England Patriots to become their new
head coach. The Jets claimed that Belichick was still under contract
with them, and in a precedent-setting move the NFL Commissioner
awarded the Jets the Patriots' first-round draft pick in 2000 in exchange
for the right to sign Belichick.

Belichick went 5–11 in his first season with the Patriots and missed
the playoffs. This was Belichick's only losing season with the Patriots,
and he has since won Super Bowls in 2001, 2002, and 2004.

His reputation was tarnished when, in 2007, a Patriots' video assistant was caught by NFL security filming the New York Jets' defensive

signals. Belichick was fined $500,000, the largest fine ever imposed on a coach in the league's history. The Patriots were also fined $250,000. In addition, the Patriots had to forfeit their first-round draft pick in the 2008 NFL draft.

Most recently, a season-ending injury to his star quarterback, Tom Brady, kept Belichick's Patriots from making it to the Super Bowl, despite having a winning record. However, he continues to be recognized as one of the most successful coaches in the NFL (Wikipedia.org; Holley, 2004).

SITUATIONAL LEADERSHIP ANALYSIS

As noted in detail in chapter 1, situational models of leadership differ from earlier trait and behavioral models in asserting that no single way of leading works in all situations. Rather, appropriate behavior depends on the circumstances at a given time. Effective managers diagnose the situation, identify the leadership style or behavior that will be most effective, and then determine whether they can implement the required style.

Bill Belichick recognized the logic of situational leadership theory early in his life. As a football player in Steve Sorota's program at Andover Prep, he compared the human resource leadership behavior exhibited by Sorota to the structural leadership behavior he observed in his father at the Naval Academy. He came to understand that each method suited the unique environment, and neither method would have worked at the other institution.

Belichick also saw the results of not being situational and being too locked into one leadership style or paradigm. In Cleveland, his manner lacked any sense of the emotions (human resource behavior) required by the team's special relationship to the city. *Sports Illustrated* writer Ned Zeman said that Belichick was ineffective in Cleveland because of "the incessant droning about how you never lighten up, about how you have all the panache of a toaster oven, and about how you're not, as they say in the NFL, 'a player's coach'" (Halberstam 2005, p. 185).

But Belichick is a quick study. Someone once asked Mary Kay Cabot, the football beat reporter for the *Cleveland Plain Dealer*, what had happened in Cleveland compared to what had happened in New England,

and she answered, "He got to make all his mistakes here and to learn from them" (Halberstam, 2005, p. 208).

When Belichick first arrived in New England as the Patriots' head coach, he soon discovered that the team he was taking over was not in good shape. He was, in fact, shocked by how much it had deteriorated in the short time since he had served as its assistant coach. There was, as he had found at Cleveland, a lack of mental and physical toughness. He knew he had to change that, but this time he was not as hard on the players as he had been in Cleveland. He learned to show patience in a difficult situation; he learned to use more human resource leadership behavior instead of depending almost exclusively on structural leadership behavior as he had in Cleveland.

Belichick was made even more aware of the situational nature of effective leadership in a conversation with Jimmy Johnson, the former coach of the Dallas Cowboys, who had won two Super Bowls in a row. After having won his first Super Bowl, Belichick was concerned about complacency setting in among his team members, preventing them from winning two in a row. In their meeting, the final point that Johnson mentioned was the danger of going back and trying to do the same things in the same way as before with the players. "They would," Johnson warned, "tune you out" (Halberstam, 2005, p. 249).

THE STRUCTURAL FRAME

Structural leaders seek to develop a new model of the relationship between structure, strategy, and environment in their organizations. Strategic planning, extensive preparation, and effecting change are priorities for them. Although there is ample evidence that Bill Belichick has utilized all the frames of leadership behavior, one could argue that he is basically a structural leader by nature. He has a reputation for being one of the very best coaches at game planning and preparing his team to execute with maximum efficiency. He actually gives his players written tests on their knowledge of the game plan. These are all traits of a structural leader.

As a structural leader, he values people taking responsibility for their own behavior. He reflects that sense of internal locus of control in much of his own behavior. Once when his New England Patriots were playing the Philadelphia Eagles, he noticed that the players were in the wrong coverage. He tried desperately to call a time-out, but he was too late, and the Eagles scored. Belichick was momentarily furious, mostly at himself, because he demands perfection first and foremost of himself. He believes that in order to expect accountability from others, one needs to practice it one's self.

Belichick's counterparts in the NFL recognize his effective structural leadership behavior. Football men, coaches and players alike, admired most about him his ability to create a *team* at a time when the outside forces working against it seemed more powerful every year and often the more talented a player was, the more he needed to display his ego and celebrate his own, rather than his team's, deeds. Belichick, as much as anyone in football, tried to limit showboating and to make the Patriots win and behave at all times like professionals.

Belichick is known for his intense and thorough preparation. For example, in preparing for the Patriot's Super Bowl appearance with the favored St. Louis Rams and their star quarterback, Kurt Warner, he began by telling his players that he had "screwed up" and done a poor job coaching last time. "I'm not going to screw up again," he promised (Halberstam, 2005, p. 48). This time, instead of focusing on the quarterback, they would focus on the Ram's great running back and receiver, Marshall Faulk. "Know where Marshall Faulk is at all times and hit him on every play, even if he doesn't have the ball" (Halberstam, 2005, p. 48). "Where is he" became the constant theme. By wearing down Marshall Faulk, the Patriots proved victorious in the end.

What had happened, Ron Jaworski, a former NFL quarterback and current television football analyst said, was not a fluke. "Belichick is the best in the game today, maybe the best ever" (Halberstam, 2005, p. 51). After eight hours of screening the Patriots/Rams film, he pronounced it "the best coaching job I've ever seen" (Halberstam, 2005, p. 50). Jaworski claims that you cannot really appreciate Bill Belichick as a coach unless you watch the game tape repeatedly. You had to do that because, otherwise, you might miss so many nuances, and "those little things would show you how he had thrown another team's timing off" (Halberstam, 2005, p. 50).

According to Maxie Baugham, the former Redskins linebacker who coached with Belichick, in addition to Belichick's work ethic and film-analysis skill learned from his father, he had what Baugham called "a great cognitive instinct" (Halberstam, 2005, p. 110). Belichick could watch the film and not only get down what each play was but, perhaps more importantly, understand what it all meant, what the *thinking* on the other side of the ball was.

In typical structural leadership style, Belichick had great confidence in his abilities. He was sure that he knew more football than his counterparts did. "I never felt I had to reach or was in an alien profession," he said (Halberstam, 2005, p. 117). He always knew he had a better instinct for the game than some of the older coaches in the league. What he didn't know, he could learn. He always felt that one of the things he had working for him was that he knew how—had a capacity—to learn. The things he had to do as an assistant and then a head coach, he could always do more quickly and clearly than those around him. Stan White, the former Colt's player, said of Belichick, "You could tell he was going to be what I call a 'forever coach,' that is, a man who is going to coach forever, because he was so good at it, so natural" (Halberstam, 2005, p. 115).

As a structural leader, Belichick fashioned himself as a strict disciplinarian. Bruce Laird, one of his defensive backs on the Colts, believes that his attitude even as a young coach was that he wasn't going to let you push him around. He was going to push you around first. He was much less skilled, for example, than Bill Parcells, with whom he worked for many years, at reaching his players emotionally and thereby challenging them to do more. This never came naturally to him; it was not who he was. In addition, he thought it was the wrong way to go, that it was too short-range, and that, in the end, one could only go to that emotional well so often before it went dry. What did fit his personality was the sum of his knowledge and being the best-prepared coach on the field. Players would do what he asked, not because he was their pal but because he could help them win, and they came to believe in his capabilities—all traits of a structural leader.

Belichick displayed another example of his structural frame leadership behavior during his interview with Cleveland Browns owner Art Modell for the head coaching position. According to Modell, Belichick showed up for his job interview, disciplined and well-prepared as ever, with everything in binders, including a year-by-year plan. He had laid out step-by-step where the Browns would be after the first year, and the second year, and the third year. There was no doubt that Belichick, more than any other candidate, had thought everything out thoroughly. He made it clear to Modell that he would be hiring a very organized workaholic.

Ray Perkins, former Giants head coach, says, "What I liked about him was his passion for the game" (Halberstam, 2005, p. 134). But it was a unique passion, according to Perkins. Belichick was very different from his coaching counterparts. He was driven by his brain power and by his fascination with the challenge that professional football represented to the mind of the coach, as well as to the bodies of the players.

In typical structural frame fashion, Belichick likes to be in control of every situation. In Cleveland, for instance, he wanted to control the media from the first, to set new rules about where they could and, more importantly, could *not* go. When Belichick first arrived in Cleveland, there had been a very open media policy from previous regimes. They had open practices, open locker rooms, pretty much whatever the media wanted, to the point where the players really had no privacy. Belichick complained that even when "a guy would play a joke on somebody or say something, it would be in the paper the next day" (Halberstam, 2005, p. 6). There was no real opportunity for the team to build much of its own chemistry because so much was reported on a daily basis.

However, he was not successful in maintaining control over the media and the players and was ultimately fired. So, Belichick decided after he left Cleveland that if he ever got another head coaching job, there would be one set of rules for everyone. He would enforce those rules uniformly with the media, and he would only sign players who had both talent and character. If there was a great player like Laurence Taylor, a unique player who created a unique problem, he would deal with it sooner rather than later.

When Belichick became head coach of the New England Patriots, therefore, he resolved to use structural leadership behavior almost exclusively, which, as we know, resulted in three Super Bowl victories. Sal Paolantonio, the ESPN football analyst said of Belichick, "If anything, he had given the football world a new definition of what a coach should be, and now everyone wanted to be 'The Next Bill Belichick'" (Halberstam, 2005, p. 269). Professionally, he could be cold and unsentimental, which the League in effect mandated in the age of the salary cap when you had to make very judicious, hard-and-fast decisions over how much you paid a player and who you could afford to keep on your team. In addition, as pointed out earlier, Cleveland had given him the hide of a rhino. If he had become a hard man, then much of that hardness was built into the job description, according to Paolantonio.

THE HUMAN RESOURCE FRAME

Human resource leaders believe in people and communicate that belief. They are passionate about *productivity through people*. Although Bill Belichick does not appear to utilize the human resource frame of leadership behavior regularly, there is evidence that he does at times see the need to include human resource behavior in his overall approach to leadership. For instance, Belichick believes that players respect coaches who can help them play better and who know things that they do not know. In his mind, that, more than anything else, defines successful player–coach relationships. Thus, he has sought opportunities to impart that knowledge on a one-on-one basis.

Belichick also knows that in order to build team chemistry, it is important to engage in human resource leadership behavior. He recalled his experience as an assistant coach with the Denver Broncos when he was beginning to build the kind of defense that he would ultimately favor in New England, featuring players who know their roles and understand that playing them is more important than being a star. Convincing players to subdue their individual egos for the good of the team requires the use of human relations leadership behavior.

After his bad experience in Cleveland, however, he became very reluctant to show the human side of his personality. Although he did not consider himself one of the league's "hard-ass" coaches—one of those men who deliberately come up with rules almost for their own sake, as if the more rules there are, the stronger the hierarchy—he did consider himself tough, and he was reluctant to let down his guard. He believed that "he had to win football games, not hearts and minds" (Halberstam, 2005, p. 271). Nevertheless, according to writer David Halberstam, who spent a great deal of time with Belichick, behind the façade was another face, which appeared when he was with family and old friends, when he could relax. "But he was reluctant to let people from the professional world into the private one" (Halberstam, 2005, p. 185).

According to Halberstam, Belichick had a sense of humor, an ironic, skeptical one, to be sure, but he saw no upside in displaying it publicly. In fact, he was convinced that it would come back to haunt him. However, if he was ultimately going to get another chance after Cleveland, his friends thought that he would surely want it to be in a situation where he felt comfortable with the owner and where he had a fair shot at developing his own program in an acceptable time frame. He did not want to be known merely as a defensive genius, a brilliant coordinator, who somehow lacked the *human skills* to be a head coach.

Ultimately, Belichick learned from his mistakes in Cleveland. Even though, when he first arrived in New England as a head coach, the players lacked mental and physical toughness, as the Cleveland team had, he was not as hard on them as he had been in Cleveland. He learned to show patience in a difficult situation. For example, after a Thanksgiving Day win in Detroit, he surprised everyone, even his assistant coaches, by giving the team the weekend off and jested, "By the way, some of you guys looked good in those red [throwback] uniforms, don't gain too much weight" (Halberstam, 2005, p. 131).

He now knew that in order to be truly effective, he had to relate to his athletes. He pointed out to them, "We need to have everybody together on this team. Now, there's not one person in this room—not one—who can't improve. And it starts with me" (Halberstam, 2005, p. 99). He pledged to sit down with any of them to show them where they could improve. Belichick finally realized that when you are head coach, you are the coach twenty-four hours a day, seven days a week. No matter what happens, it will be perceived as the coach's responsibility. Even if players get involved in criminal activity, it somehow becomes the coach's responsibility. Given this reality, Belichick knew he had to exhibit at least of modicum of human resource behavior.

Belichick even engaged in human resource behavior with the media, as Joan Vennochi, a political columnist, wrote. "Belichick wasn't glib or glitzy. At press conferences he sometimes seems a little goofy and is often way too grim." However, according to Vennochi, he is a leader without the swagger, selfishness, and pomposity that so many men in business, politics, and sports embrace as an entitlement of their gender and position.

THE SYMBOLIC FRAME

In the symbolic frame, the organization is seen as a stage, a theater in which every actor plays certain roles, and the symbolic leader attempts to communicate the right impressions to the right audiences. Although the symbolic frame is not one that Bill Belichick focuses on, evidence suggests that he does see the need to utilize symbolic frame leadership when appropriate. For example, in his four years as an assistant coach with the New York Giants, he began the process of becoming the Bill Belichick of the NFL who would finally surface in the media: ultrastudious, a workaholic, without much sense of humor. He did not have a light touch, especially with the general public; he was there to know the answers, often before the players had the questions. That persona—the Belichick who had been born thirty years old—was one he had either created for the NFL or evolved because of what he viewed as the contemporary game's needs. According to author Halberstam, "Part of the design was more or less deliberate, and part of it was who he was" (Halberstam, 2005, p. 157).

The "face" seemed to reflect a certain wariness that both came with the man and went with the job—the face of someone on guard. The face also seemed to reflect a belief that if you relaxed too much, someone—owner, players, reporter, stranger—would take advantage of you. Unveiling one's emotions might be seen as a weakness, so Belichick was loath to do so.

Belichick saw himself in this stoic image to the point where he contrasted his leadership behavior with those who saw football in a different light. For example, his boss, Cleveland Browns owner Art Modell, made his fortune in marketing. Belichick considered Modell to be in the "sizzle" business, while he was in the "steak" business—and he had contempt for those who were in the sizzle business (Halberstam, 2005, p. 179).

THE POLITICAL FRAME

Leaders operating out of the political frame clarify what they want and what they can get. Political leaders are realists above all. They never let what they want cloud their judgment about what is possible. They assess the distribution of power and interests. It is safe to say that all football coaches utilize political frame leadership behavior at some point in their careers. Negotiating—be it with general managers in salary matters, with the front office in personnel decisions, or with players regarding playing time—is a commonly used practice among football coaches, and Bill Belichick is no exception to the rule.

An example of Belichick's use of raw power occurred during his first Super Bowl appearance with the New England Patriots. It had been NFL tradition to introduce the defensive unit of one team and the offensive unit of the other in pregame introductions. Belichick insisted that *both* units be introduced. The NFL resisted at first but eventually capitulated when Belichick made an issue of it.

Another example of Belichick's use of the political frame was in replacing Bernie Kosar as his quarterback in his first head coaching job with the Cleveland Browns. Kosar had been a huge local celebrity, a kind of "Mr. Cleveland." In effect, Belichick ended up "running against him." In a battle of wills, Kosar was finally replaced by Vinnie Testaverde, but Cleveland fans held the change against Belichick. "The brutality of the way it was done was unacceptable," according to Halberstam (Halberstam, 2005, p. 191). Belichick thought he was just doing his job, but he had been mistaken; he had defined his job too narrowly and not utilized the political frame of leadership effectively.

But Belichick learned from his mistakes. In effect, he had gone from a twenty-six-year-old coach-peer to a fifty-four-year-old coach-teacher. He learned to be more of a negotiator with his team, making compromises in some areas—or at least demonstrating an ability to listen—without compromising his core beliefs. He said, "I clamped down on them. It could have been done in a more positive and gracious way. I could have made some concessions so that it wouldn't come off as being so harsh. I take responsibility for that" (Halberstam, 2005, p. 6).

An incident in which Matt Light, a Patriots offensive tackle, asked for a day off in the dog days of training camp in August provides an example of how Belichick's use of political frame behavior evolved. Belichick was loath to give into the request without some type of "trade-off" and insisted on a quid pro quo. He told Light and the team that they could have a day off if Light could catch a punt. Obviously, an offensive tackle is not trained to field punts, so Light had to put in a tremendous amount of effort to learn how to catch a punt before the day of reckoning. With his teammates standing around as the punt went into the air, Light was under enormous pressure. If he caught the ball, he and his teammates would have a day off. If not, they would have a full practice. After he caught the punt, his teammates cheered as if they had just won the Super Bowl. It then became an annual tradition at preseason camp.

Nevertheless, Belichick was not as creative in his use of political frame behavior if his character was being challenged. When Belichick was being fired by the Cleveland Browns, Art Modell's proposed firing statement was very harsh and one-sided. "If you release this statement, I'm going to release one, and you're not going to like it," said Belichick. "So, let's try to come up with something that we can both live with" (Halberstam, 2005, p. 8). They did.

CONCLUSION

Although Bill Belichick can be described as basically a structural frame leader because of his effective and extensive use of structural frame leadership behavior, ample evidence shows that, when appropriate, he infuses his leadership behavior with practices emblematic of the other three Bolman-Deal leadership frames. Reputedly one of the best-prepared coaches in the National Football League, he is recognized especially for his ability to develop an effective game plan. He is considered an expert at analyzing game films, a skill that he learned from his father, Steve, a former NFL player and assistant coach. Of course, these attributes are characteristic of a structural frame leader. Unfortunately, as noted earlier, his reputation as a game film analyst was tarnished in the 2007 season when he was found to be illegally filming the opposing team's signals.

He is also known as a "football genius," an image that he cultivates with the subtle use of symbolic frame leadership behavior. And although he does so sparingly, he utilizes human resource frame leadership behavior where and when appropriate. Finally, he has strong views about how the business of football should be run and sometimes uses political frame behavior to make his point. Overall, we can see that Bill Belichick's reputation as an effective leader has been well earned. Although one could argue that he would be more effective if he utilized one of the other leadership frames more extensively, in general, he places situational leadership theory into effective practice in an exemplary way.

4

BOBBY BOWDEN

If you're going to sin, sin boldly.

—Martin Luther

BACKGROUND

Born in 1929, Bobby Bowden is the head football coach at Florida State University. Since assuming the position in 1976, Bowden has led FSU to National Championships in 1993 and 1999, as well as to thirteen Atlantic Coast Conference championships.

His more than 375 career victories place him along side Joe Paterno as the all-time winningest Division I coach in history. Bowden was an outstanding football player at Woodlawn High School in Birmingham, Alabama. He then went on to play quarterback at the University of Alabama.

Having served as an assistant football coach and head track-and-field coach at Howard College (now Samford University) in 1954 and 1955, he left to become athletic director and head football, baseball, and basketball coach at South Georgia College from 1956 to 1958. Bowden then returned to Howard as head coach, where he compiled a 31–6 record in four years. His success at Howard earned him an offer to go to Florida State University as an assistant coach under Bill Peterson. After three years, he left to go to West Virginia University as assistant coach. When the head coach at West Virginia left before the 1970 season, Bowden replaced him. Bowden compiled a 42–26 record at West Virginia University before returning to FSU as head coach in 1976.

In his thirty-two years as the head coach at FSU, he has had but one losing season, his first. His most recent FSU teams have enjoyed sixteen straight seasons with ten or more wins. Florida State finished an unprecedented fourteen straight seasons in the top five of the Associated Press College Football Poll and won two National Championships. One of Bowden's greatest coaching achievements is his success in postseason bowl games. His 20–8–1 record ranks second to Joe Paterno, who is also profiled in this book.

Bobby Bowden is joined by his three sons as Division I football coaches. Until recently, his son Tommy Bowden was the head coach at Clemson University. Another son, Terry Bowden, was the head coach at Auburn University where he was the 1993 Coach of the Year. A third son, Jeff Bowden, was the offensive coordinator at Florida State. Three of the Bowdens have achieved an undefeated season: Terry in 1993 at Auburn, Tommy in 1998 at Tulane, and Bobby in 1999 at Florida State. Bobby's 1993 and 1999 Florida State teams were the only ones to win a National Championship, however. Since Florida State and Clemson are in the same division of the Atlantic Coast Conference for football, the two teams play every year in a game that has become known as "the Bowden Bowl." Bobby Bowden was inducted into the College Football Hall of Fame in 2006 and continues to be one of the oldest and most successful coaches in college football (Bowden, 2001; La Monte & Shook, 2004; Wikipedia.org).

SITUATIONAL LEADERSHIP ANALYSIS

Situational leadership models differ from the earlier trait and behavioral models in asserting that no single way of leading works in all situations. Rather, appropriate behavior depends on the circumstances at a given time. Effective managers diagnose the situation, identify the leadership style or behavior that will be most effective, and then determine whether they can implement the required style.

In Bobby Bowden's long career as a football coach, his recognition of the situational nature of effective leadership behavior has definitely enhanced his effectiveness as a leader. He points out that from a purely practical standpoint, the need to adjust one's leadership behavior to the situation makes perfect sense. For example, like most head coaches, Bowden delegates much of the teaching responsibility to his assistants. Their basic leadership styles may be different from his but he believes that he "must allow for those differences" because their styles may be more effective in their unique situations (Bowden 2001, p. 120) In fact, he acknowledges that in given situations, their approaches might indeed be more effective than his because he does not have the same relationship with the players that they do.

Bowden believes that he has a fair grasp of human nature. Some people will be as lazy as you allow them to be. Stern measures are the only way to reform them. On the other hand, most people will do the right thing most of the time. "They need to be handled more gently," according to Bowden (Bowden, 2001, p. 125).

In a further acknowledgment of the situational nature of leadership behavior, Bowden observes that when he first started his career, he was a strict disciplinarian. It was, "Yes, sir," "No, sir," short hair, no tattoos, no earrings, and absolutely no disrespect toward himself or his coaches. It was "definitely my way or the highway" (Bowden, 2001, p. 127). But as his career passed through the 1940s, 1950s, 1960s, and now the new millennium, he eased up somewhat, except in regard to morality and his personal ideals. There is a colloquialism that if you hold a bird in your hand too tightly, you will kill it, but if you hold it too loosely, it will fly away. "I squeezed a little too tightly in my younger years," he declares (Bowden, 2001, p. 127). As Bowden observes, "If short haircuts and polite manners were the keys to success, Army and Navy would play for the National Championship every year" (Bowden, 2001, p. 233).

An incident involving three of his greatest players, Laveranues Coles, Randy Moss, and Peter Warwick, demonstrates specifically how Bowden altered his leadership behavior according to the situation. It seems that a sporting-goods store clerk, knowing who they were, sold them merchandise at an unauthorized, exorbitantly discounted rate. When Bowden found out about it, he punished all three players, but he punished Coles and Moss more severely than Warwick. Of course, he was accused of playing favorites. However, Coles and Moss had been in trouble before, whereas Warwick was a first-time offender. Thus, Bowden adjusted his leadership behavior to apply to the different situations.

Bowden explains the evolution of his thinking regarding the situational nature of leadership by referring to his imitation of the coaching greats of his era: Frank Leahy at Notre Dame, Bear Bryant at Alabama, and Tom Dodd at Georgia Tech. Any coach worth his salt during that era taught "smash-mouth" football. But by 1963, Bill Peterson had hired Bowden as an assistant at Florida State, and he taught "finesse" football and the passing game. He did so because of the situation. They had a team that could not compete physically, so they used deception and passed when most teams ran. In effect, they adjusted their leadership behavior to the situation at hand.

Finally, Bowden points out that one of his current assistant coaches at Florida State is in the Bear Bryant mold. As a result, he is very intense during practice, and his emotional demeanor carries over onto the sidelines during a game. He's a perfectionist who demands the absolute best from his players. However, sometimes Bowden has to play the good guy to his bad guy to mollify the players and preclude a negative reaction from them—another example of the value of adjusting one's leadership behavior to the situation.

THE STRUCTURAL FRAME

Structural leaders seek to develop a new model of the relationship between structure, strategy, and environment in their organizations. Strategic planning, extensive preparation, and effecting change are priorities for them. Coach Bowden definitely utilizes structural frame leadership behavior in his overall leadership style. Bowden considers football to be a great teacher. It thrust him into a leadership role before he felt ready to lead, and it proved a harsh taskmaster—at times testing his convictions, punishing his mistakes, and relentlessly pushing him beyond what he thought were his capabilities. Still, football taught him more about leadership than he could have otherwise learned.

Bowden learned that "the dynamics of leadership don't change much when we shift from the football field to the corporate board room, the sales manager's office, or the principal's office" (Bowden, 2001, p. xi). One must work with others, and thereby lead them, to conceive, implement, and maintain a successful plan—and successful planning is the key to success. This is typical structural frame thinking.

In addition to drawing from his own experience regarding the need for structural leadership behavior, Bowden has long been a student of military history. He pores over biographies of well-known generals of the modern era, all great leaders who accomplished great things on the battlefield, including Napoleon Bonaparte, Ulysses S. Grant, Robert E. Lee, Stonewall Jackson, George S. Patton, Erwin Rommel, Dwight D. Eisenhower, and Douglas MacArthur. Bowden concludes that building a successful program boils down to accomplishing four objectives:

1. devising a good game plan (preparation),
2. hiring good people to implement the plan,
3. motivating players and other personnel to buy into the plan, and
4. executing the plan (Bowden, 2001, p. 3).

Like many other structural frame leaders, Bowden is a known as a workaholic. Mostly, he works fourteen- to sixteen-hour days, sometimes seven days a week. He is a self-described stickler for detail and fine-tunes his plans each year. He expects his staff to buy into the program's goals and be on the same page regarding their particular assignments, responsibilities, and expectations. He schedules what he calls a "hideaway" each year at the end of July for strategic and tactical planning.

Having engaged in these preliminaries, he feels secure in empowering his coaches to deal with certain problems and issues on their own, trusting their judgment and giving them his support. He suggests that "we work like this is the last job we will ever have and live like it's the last day of our lives" (Bowden, 2001, p. 65).

In typical structural frame leadership style, Bowden has "mat drills" at 6 a.m., which are winter conditioning drills. "We build our team on those mats," he says (Bowden, 2001, p. 8). Players push one another not to drag behind. If a drill is not performed properly by any individual, the entire team must repeat it. And during the process, Bowden discovers who the natural leaders are, which players work the hardest and have the ability to influence others to keep up.

Like a true structural leader, Bowden believes that players play the way they practice. He suggests that we take advantage of the teachable moments at practice and elsewhere to assume the role of leader and share our vision for the future. Lay the ground rules that all must follow and enumerate your expectations, letting the players see your resolve to move the organization in the right direction.

Bowden is known for running a "clean" program at Florida State; that is, he does not engage in questionable recruiting practices. He is intent on playing by the rules and offering prospective student athletes a full scholarship and nothing more. Drug abuse, academic negligence, dissension, stealing, lying, and committing a major crime will get a player dismissed from the team. Laziness, cheating, immorality, and illegal activity will get an assistant coach fired. His strong positions on immorality and ethics violations spring from his equally strong religious convictions. However, in true structural leader fashion, Bowden says, "If I must fire someone or dismiss a player, I view that dismissal as my failure" (Bowden, 2001, p. 99).

In true structural frame fashion, he attends every practice with a note card and a pen in his back pocket. He sits up in a tall tower so that he can watch everything going on—and the players can see him looming like "big brother." He doesn't have a plethora of rules, but those that he has, he enforces strictly, applying them equally and fairly. He prides himself on not playing favorites.

Bowden is a devotee of Total Quality Management (TQM), which stresses the team approach to producing high-quality products and services. He derives what he calls "Bowden's Principles" from this approach to management (Bowden, 2001, p. 138). Among his principles is the practice of praying together before and after games, delegating responsibilities, encouraging independent thinking, not criticizing players and coaches in public, not engaging in emotional outbursts, explaining why things are done in a certain way, and empowering the players to take leadership roles. Finally, he believes in the TQM principle of continuous progress, which implies continuous change. Bowden points out that the Bible says, "Fear not," which is a good starting point for any leader or aspiring leader (Bowden, 2001, p. 234).

According to Bowden, complacency is the greatest threat to continuous progress. He also believes that players play the way they practice. He uses the 1972 Peach Bowl as an example to make his point. It was Florida State versus Lou Holtz's North Carolina State team. Bowden let his players celebrate a great season and loosened the reins during the week spent in Atlanta preparing for the Peach Bowl. As a result, his Florida State team was embarrassed 49–13. He learned his lesson about complacency being the enemy of continuous progress. "Just because you've learned to drive doesn't mean you take your hands off the wheel," he declares (Bowden, 2001, p. 217).

THE HUMAN RESOURCE FRAME

Human resource leaders believe in people and communicate that belief. They are passionate about *productivity through people*. Bobby Bowden is a very people-oriented person. Abundant evidence shows that he truly values the use of the human resource frame of leadership behavior and practices it with great frequency. He tries to treat his players the same way that he treated his children when they were young. "You discipline your kids, but you don't throw them to the wolves," he says (Bowden, 2001, p. 50). For example, when considering whether to dismiss a player from the team, he continually asks himself which option is in the player's best interest: to keep him on the team, discipline him, and continue to monitor him or to "throw him on the street" and wash your hands of him (Bowden, 2001, p. 52). He cautions us not to forget that some of those boys come from broken homes, poor families, and rough neighborhoods. He reminds himself that every player's mother is hoping that he will take care of her son while he is at FSU. Bowden points to one of his players, Todd Williams, whose father rejected him at birth. He lived with relatives and was suspended from high school several times. However, he stayed the course and made a name for himself as a player and graduate of Florida State. If we can affect even one Todd Williams in our lifetimes, we will have done a great service to humanity, Bowden concludes.

Bowden also extends his human resource behavior to other situations. For example, it is commonplace for college coaches to change players' positions after they are recruited, depending on the needs of the team and the player's capabilities. However, Bowden has a policy of not simply informing the player that he will play a different position. He asks the player what he thinks about his reasons for making the change, and if the player disagrees, "we leave him be" (Bowden, 2001, p. 41). Bowden concludes that the major reason FSU players push themselves harder than players at many other schools is because "they know their coaches care for them and support them" (Bowden, 2001, p. 61).

He also tells his players' parents that he will watch over their sons while they are at FSU. According to Bowden, parents have a natural anxiety about their child's departure from home. In their minds, many bad things can happen to them on today's college campuses. He conveys his sincere aim to watch over their young men, providing them with a good environment in which to obtain an education and protecting them from certain dangers they might confront. Bowden believes that nothing wins trust like a good track record. "If I can demonstrate to parents that I'm a man who keeps his word, they will trust me with their most precious possession, their child" (Bowden, 2001, p. 87).

Bowden knows that projecting the image of a strong disciplinarian is the preferred position in many circles. "Kicking a boy off the team" is a very popular thing to do. The alums can say, "Look how tough our coach is." But it's often the wrong thing to do, according to Bowden. "I don't mind being unpopular, if that's the consequence of *caring* for my players" (Bowden, 2001, p. 130). To make his point, Bowden cites an incident where Joe Paterno's starting quarterback at Penn State was accused of assault and battery. Paterno stood by the player in the face of the alumni and others calling for extreme measures. Ultimately, the player was found not guilty in a court of law. "Now, you tell me how you think the football players at Penn State feel about Joe Paterno" (Bowden, 2001, p. 211).

THE SYMBOLIC FRAME

In the symbolic frame, the organization is seen as a stage, a theater in which every actor plays certain roles, and the symbolic leader attempts to communicate the right impressions to the right audiences. Like many of his counterparts in coaching, Bobby Bowden is quite astute at using symbolic leadership behavior.

Bobby Bowden very consciously projects the image of a principled leader. Although many of his career accomplishments are unparalleled and have been achieved under remarkable circumstances, he is praised as much for his moral convictions as for his professional achievements. Bowden often refers to his strong religious beliefs to make his points. We began this chapter with one of his favorite quotes. The Protestant reformer Martin Luther once said, "If you're going to sin, sin boldly" (Bowden, 2001, p. 18). Bowden's interpretation of this quote might read, "If you're going to be wrong, be wrong decisively." Just don't repeat your mistake. Bowden believes that the fear of making bad decisions has paralyzed many a prospective leader.

He defends his choice in leadership style by contrasting his more human resource–oriented image to the more structurally oriented image of the legendary Bear Bryant of Alabama. As a leader, you should always be yourself, he advises. Twenty-nine former Bear Bryant assistants went on to become head coaches, but twenty-seven of them got fired. Bowden believes that you can learn from a coach like Bryant, but you can't be *like* him, no matter how hard you try. Each person must be him- or herself. As for Bowden, he prefers to lead with a baton rather than a big stick.

In true symbolic leadership fashion, Bowden believes in the importance of serving as an exemplar for his players. He does not believe in the old adage "Do as I say, not as I do." According to Bowden, if you want to lead, you have to lead by example. Whatever you expect from others, they had better see it first in you, he advises. Along these lines, he sets two "integrity" rules for himself: (1) don't say anything you don't want repeated in public because it probably will be, and (2) don't do anything you don't mind everyone knowing about because they eventually will. Thus, he urges his players to join him in accepting their responsibility as role models. The fact that they are role models is, in Bowden's mind, "a fact of life" (Bowden, 2001, p. 27).

Bowden proudly cites one of his former star players, Charlie Ward, as an example of his program's influence. As Bowden sees it, his former quarterback was one of the best role models his program at FSU has ever produced. Ward, the 1993 Heisman Trophy winner, decided on a career in professional basketball rather than football and ended up playing for the tough and nasty New York Knicks. However, he mollified that image by starting the practice of leading a prayer at the end of the Knicks games, win or lose, that still goes on today.

According to Bowden, integrity in the form of trust and respect is the glue that holds the pieces together, and it must begin with the leader. If one expects his decisions to be accepted, especially the difficult ones, his followers need to believe in the leader's integrity. For example, two of Bowden's most famous players, Warrick Dunn and Deion Sanders, were great high school quarterbacks but were asked to change positions. Bowden believes that they never would have accepted the change if they had not trusted the coaching staff.

Bowden consciously projects the image of humility rather than arrogance. In fact, he admits a preference for going "head-to-head" with an arrogant adversary on the football field because chances are an arrogant individual will be blind to some of his weaknesses. Bowden recalls an experience of competing against an arrogant coach when he had Tamarick Vanover as his All-American punt returner at FSU. If Bowden had been coaching against his own team, he would have kicked away from Vanover, but his opposing coach was so arrogant, he kicked to Vanover and depended on his great coaching to stop him. Vanover returned two punts for touchdowns and almost single handedly won the game for FSU.

Bowden used symbolic leadership behavior to project the image of a good family man. Because of the long hours that coaching demands, he always looked for ways to blend family life with work and encouraged his assistants to do likewise. For example, his sons attended games, home and away, and he often brought his daughters on recruiting trips with him.

Another image that Bowden works hard to project is the importance of religious beliefs in a leader's life. He has established a tradition of beginning every staff meeting with a devotional and a prayer. His coaches and trainers are asked to take turns leading. The devotionals are limited to two to three minutes, and personal anecdotes are encouraged. To demonstrate the impact that these devotionals can have, Bowden recalls an incident regarding Dr. Tom Osborne, the legendary Nebraska football coach. Osborne just couldn't win the national championship after coming close many times. In 1994, he asked Bowden if he could attend FSU's practices for a week. Nebraska won three of the next four national championships. When asked what led to this success, Osborne responded that the only difference between his and FSU's practices had been the devotionals, and once he instituted them at Nebraska, they started winning the "big ones" (Bowden, 2001, p. 112). Bowden truly believes that a genuine faith has an enormous impact on the way people work together and with their players.

However, Bowden humorously recollects when other's use of symbolic behavior has not always been so complimentary. He recalls that when he was at Alabama, the bumper stickers read "Beat Auburn." When he was at West Virginia, they read "Beat Pitt." When he first came to FSU, the bumper stickers read "Beat Anybody." He also pointed out that when he is winning, the fans call him "Sweet Ol' Bobby." When he is losing, they just abbreviate the name (Bowden, 2001, p. 193).

THE POLITICAL FRAME

Leaders operating out of the political frame clarify what they want and what they can get. Political leaders are realists above all. They never let what they want cloud their judgment about what is possible. They assess the distribution of power and interests and behave accordingly. Bobby Bowden describes a number of instances when he utilized political frame leadership behavior. As a leader, Bowden agrees that a football coach sometimes has to be the "mouthpiece for the organization. The public is eager to know what the coach has to say. They assume that the coach knows more about the team and the university than most others. Bowden says that "salesmanship is a major component of modern college football" (Bowden, 2001, p. 81). FSU boosters and alumni, high school coaches, and even the players are the audience.

Another instance of Bowden's use of political frame leadership behavior is with the media. He notes that sportswriters are the medium of communication between the coach and the public. Thus, especially in his early years, he granted interviews whenever asked. And he made certain that he was never perceived as being argumentative with the media, aloof from the general public, at odds with his players, or prone to bouts of bad temper. He adds, however, "It ain't that way anymore" (Bowden, 2001, p. 79). Too many people wanted him to be in too many places before and after practice to the point where it became a distraction. He preferred to use that time watching film and preparing for the next game. He found that such infringements cannot entirely be avoided, but he learned to deal with them as efficiently as possible, sometimes having to deny requests for interviews and access.

CONCLUSION

Bobby Bowden displays a very appropriate balance in his leadership behavior. He obviously sees the need to utilize the broad range of leadership behaviors in order to maximize his effectiveness. He uses structural frame behavior in preparing his teams to consistently reach peak performance, while utilizing human resource leadership behavior to motivate them to function as a team rather than as a collection of individuals. His symbolic leadership behavior is primarily based on his strong religious values and his belief that he and his student athletes should serve as role models. Finally, he acknowledges the need to engage in political frame leadership behavior on occasion. He works hard to place FSU in the best possible light. In summary, Bobby Bowden has much to offer to leaders and aspiring leaders who wish to apply situational leadership theory to their leadership behavior.

⑤

BEAR BRYANT

Winning isn't everything, but it beats anything that comes in second.

—Bear Bryant

BACKGROUND

Born in 1913, Paul "Bear" Bryant was best known as the longtime head football coach of the University of Alabama. Before Alabama, Bryant was head coach at the University of Maryland, the University of Kentucky, and Texas A&M University. Bryant's nickname stemmed from his having agreed to wrestle a bear on a dare during a carnival when he was thirteen years old. He attended Fordyce High School in Arkansas. As a senior, the team won the 1930 Arkansas state football championship.

As a result of his high school success, Bryant was awarded a scholarship to play for the University of Alabama in 1931. Bryant played end for the Crimson Tide and played on the school's 1934 National Championship team.

In 1936, after high school graduation, Bryant took an assistant coaching position at his alma mater. After four years, he left to become an assistant at Vanderbilt University. Following the 1941 season, Bryant joined the U.S. Navy. He served in North Africa, but saw no combat action. However his ship, the USS *Uruguay*, was rammed by another vessel and ordered to be abandoned. Bryant, an officer, disobeyed the order, and in doing so, saved the lives of his men. He was granted an honorable discharge to train recruits and coach the football team at a Naval Base in North Carolina. One of the players he coached in the navy was Otto Graham, who later became the great Cleveland Browns quarterback under the legendary coach, Paul Brown.

Bryant was appointed head coach at the University of Maryland in 1945. In his only season with the Maryland Terrapins, Bryant led the team to a 6–2–1 record. However, there was a personality clash between Bryant and Harry Clifton "Curley" Byrd. Byrd was a former Maryland coach, and when Bryant was coach, he was the university president. In a widely publicized event Bryant suspended a player for violating team rules only to discover that Byrd had the player reinstated while Bryant was away on vacation. As a result, Bryant left Maryland to take over the head coaching position at the University of Kentucky.

For the next eight seasons, Bryant coached at the University of Kentucky. Under Bryant, Kentucky made its first bowl appearance and won its first Southeastern Conference (SEC) title. The 1950 Kentucky team concluded its season with a victory over Bud Wilkinson's top-ranked University of Oklahoma Sooners in the Sugar Bowl. As a result, many of the national media agreed they should have won the National Championship.

In 1954 Bryant became the head coach and athletic director at Texas A&M. At the close of the 1957 season, having compiled an overall 25–14–2 record at A&M, Bryant returned to his alma mater to take the head coaching and athletic director positions at Alabama.

Bryant's career at Alabama became legendary. After winning a total of four games in the previous three years, the Crimson Tide went 5–4–1 in Bryant's first season. The next year, Alabama appeared in a bowl game for the first time in six years. In 1961, Alabama had an undefeated season and defeated Arkansas in the Sugar Bowl to claim the national championship.

In 1962, Joe Namath began to make his mark at Alabama. His first season ended with a victory in the Orange Bowl over Bud Wilkinson's Oklahoma Sooners. In 1964, the Tide won another National Championship. Then they took the championship again in 1965 after defeat-ing Nebraska in the Orange Bowl. Coming off back-to-back national championship seasons, Bryant's Alabama team went undefeated again in 1966 and defeated Nebraska in the Sugar Bowl. However, despite be-ing undefeated, Alabama finished third in the nation behind Michigan State and Notre Dame.

Bryant coached at Alabama for twenty-five years, winning six national titles and thirteen SEC championships. Bryant announced his retire-ment as head football coach at Alabama at the end of the 1982 season. His last game was a victory over Illinois in the Liberty Bowl. When asked in a postgame interview what he intended to do in retirement, Bryant replied sarcastically that he would "probably croak in a week." Unfortunately, his prediction came true. He passed away only twenty-eight days after his last game as coach. He was inducted into the College Football Hall of Fame in 1986 (Bryant & Underwood, 1974; La Monte & Shook, 2004; Wikipedia.org).

SITUATIONAL LEADERSHIP ANALYSIS

Situational leadership models differ from the earlier trait and behavioral models in asserting that no single way of leading works in all situations. Rather, appropriate behavior depends on the circumstances at a given time. Effective managers diagnose the situation, identify the leader-ship style or behavior that will be most effective, and then determine whether they can implement the required style.

Although Bear Bryant had a reputation as a strong structural frame leader, evidence in his coaching behavior leads us to believe that he was at least aware of the "situationalness" of effective leadership behavior. In contrasting his leadership style with that of his coaching colleague and good friend Bobby Dodd, the former coach of Georgia Tech Uni-versity, Bryant acknowledges that varying one's leadership behavior de-pending on the situation works. Bryant described his style as practicing hard, playing hard, and winning, whereas Dodd was known for his easy training program and "all those between-meal snacks and water breaks, and playing volleyball instead of scrimmaging" (Bryant 1974, p. 9). But Dodd was one of the best in-game strategists of his time and won games because he outmaneuvered opponents and placed his skilled players in the best possible positions during a game to maximize their ability. By his own admission, Bryant was far less successful at that.

Bryant tried to teach sacrifice and physical and mental discipline to his coaches and players. But there were times when, according to Bryant, he went too far, asked too much, and took out his own mistakes on them. "I lost games by overworking my teams, and I lost some good boys by pushing them too far, or by being pigheaded" (Bryant, 1974, p. 10).

Bryant learned that the same leadership behavior does not necessarily yield the same results in every situation. For example, when trying to motivate John David Crow, his All-American halfback, to work harder in practice, he used structural frame behavior and threatened to cut him from the team. Crow responded by begging Bryant to keep him, promising to practice harder if he did. But when he approached another of his sulking players using the same tactic, volunteering to "help him pack," this player actually *let* Bryant help him and ended up transferring to another school where he became an All-American, then went on to play six years for the Cleveland Browns in the National Football League (Bryant, 1974, p. 13).

According to Bryant, young people change all the time. His football players changed too, and as a result, so did he. For example, he allowed his Alabama players to wear their hair long, whereas at Kentucky and Texas A&M, he did not. He said that he did not lose his convictions during the 1960s but realized that since he was dealing with a different "situation" during that era, he needed to adjust his leadership behavior accordingly. He began using more human resource–oriented behavior. He came to realize a truism in leadership in this situation: "anything that is important to the kids is *important*" (Bryant, 1974, p. 15).

Bryant learned that those who do not vary their leadership behavior will cease to be effective. For example, Bryant did not consider himself a big "hell-raiser" at practice. He didn't think any coach could consistently berate his players and be effective. If the coach "whoops and hollers" all the time, the players will get used to it and eventually tune the coach out. Thus, Bryant did not strive for "sameness"; he strove for "balance." He believed that kids are different, and because of that, you want different personalities around them. They cannot all relate to one type of personality. On the coaching end, Bryant felt that there were blackboard coaches and field coaches, and a rare few were both. With some it was never how much they knew but how much they could teach. One's ability to adjust one's leadership behavior is particularly important in college coaching because the cast of characters changes at least once every four years.

Finally, Bryant also realized that how the coach interacts with the team as a whole may differ from how he interacts with the individuals comprising it. The leader must analyze the team mentality and apply the appropriate leadership behavior. Likewise, the coach needs to know each individual on the team so as to apply the leadership behavior that will best motivate him. Bryant believed that "you have to learn what makes this or that Sammy run." For some, it's a pat on the back; for another, it's chewing him out; for still another, it's a fatherly talk. "You're a fool, if you think as I did as a young coach, that you can treat them all alike" (Bryant, 1974, p. 195).

THE STRUCTURAL FRAME

Structural leaders seek to develop a new model of the relationship between structure, strategy, and environment in their organizations. Strategic planning, extensive preparation, and effecting change are priorities for them. Bear Bryant was known for his extensive use of structural frame leadership behavior. He was a strict disciplinarian who drilled mental and physical toughness into his players. To him, "time is wasted if you sleep past 6 a.m." (Bryant, 1974, p. 7).

Bryant always believed that an inferior team could beat a superior team with "just plain conditioning" (Bryant, 1974, p. 19). If he was having a bad practice, he was not above sending the team back into the locker room, clearing the field of spectators, and bringing the team back out and practicing until they got serious, no matter how long it took. Bryant was determined that he was going to outwork everybody, and he worked day and night, talking with people about football, sitting home hours by himself working on strategy, and going on recruiting trips himself, rather than depending on his assistants. One of his star players, George Blanda, once said of Bryant, "Playing for him was like going to war. You may come out intact, but you'll never forget the experience" (Bryant, 1974, p. 95).

Bryant believed that if hard-nosed, even brutal football would get a player to discipline himself, get him into such keen physical condition that he would make fewer mistakes than his opponent who wasn't so well conditioned, then he was in favor of it. If it took getting into his infamous "pit" to do it, he'd "get in there with them" (Bryant, 1974, p. 183). Bryant once figured out that after the time spent in huddles and the other nonplaying time is eliminated, there is actually less than six minutes of action in a game. Any kid who could not put out for six minutes, according to Bryant, had "to be stupid or some kind of dog" (Bryant, 1974, p. 191).

However, Bryant knew that his way was not the only way. He always advised young coaches—or corporate executives and bank presidents—that leaders should not try to remake players in their own image. He made sure that his assistants didn't look alike, think alike, or have the same personalities, so that they could relate better with the players' differing personalities.

As a structural leader, Bryant placed much effort into game preparation and strategy. He once was able to predict every play that a Georgia Tech quarterback would run because of what he had observed in previous game films. If the quarterback's feet were parallel to the line, he was going to hand off. If one foot was behind the other, it was a pass, and which foot was to the rear indicated the direction he was going to throw. With these kinds of insights, Bryant's teams became very successful.

In true structural leader fashion, Bryant was as tough on himself as he was on his team. In referring to a game with Tennessee that ended in a tie, Bryant was more disappointed with his own performance than that of the team. He told the team that if he had it to do over, he would stay home and just send the team to Birmingham. He insisted that they would have won if he had not been there to make the mistakes that he had made. He said it was the most disorganized bench, the most disorganized game plan, and "the most disorganized everything I've ever seen" (Bryant, 1974, p. 271).

As with most structural leaders, Bryant stressed the importance of consistency and fairness. When asked early in his career if he treated his black and white players alike, he said that he treated everyone alike. However, later in his career, he realized that treating everyone equally does not necessarily mean that one is treating everyone fairly. He noted that he had to apply different measures to each player, depending not on their race but on their individual needs. One you pat on the back, and he'll jump out the window for you. Another you kick in the tail. A third you yell and scream at a little. But the bottom line is that you have to be fair. "And that's what I am" (Bryant, 1974, p. 306).

Still, Bryant believed that you win with preparation, dedication, and "plain old desire" (Bryant, 1974, p. 327). If you've got eleven on the field, and they beat the other eleven physically, they will win. The other team will start making mistakes in the fourth quarter, and the best-prepared and -conditioned team will ultimately prevail.

Bryant considered himself a student of the game. He believed that if one wishes to make a living by coaching football, one has no alternative but to know the game thoroughly. But he also believed that formations and strategies will not win games in and of themselves. You need talented players, and you have to motivate them. According to Bryant, you must have all three elements: knowledge, players with talent, and the ability to motivate them to reach their potential. All of these concepts are endemic to a situational leader who recognizes the need to utilize a variety of leadership frames but retains a preference for structural frame behavior.

THE HUMAN RESOURCE FRAME

Human resource leaders believe in people and communicate that belief. They are passionate about *productivity through people*. Although this frame is not Bear Bryant's primary focus, a number of instances can be cited in which he acknowledges the necessity of applying human resource leadership behavior to certain situations in order to be effective. For instance, when Bum Philips, his former player and assistant coach, was asked to describe Bryant, he indicated that Bryant doesn't coach football; he coaches people. According to Philips, "Bryant can take his'n and beat your'n and take your'n and beat his'n" (Bryant, 1974, p. viii). Obviously, Philips considers Bryant to be a supreme motivator—an ingredient that he believed separates the winners from the losers—in football and in life.

Many observers would consider Bryant the insensitive type, but he admitted to crying all the way to College Station the night the NCAA put his Texas A&M team on probation and again when he had to suspend the greatest athlete he ever saw, Joe Namath, with two games left in the season. He also "cried like a baby" when he had to tell his Aggie players that he was leaving for Alabama. Finally, he cried privately over what he considered to be the dirtiest journalism ever, when the *Saturday Evening Post* accused Bryant and Wally Butts of fixing the Georgia/Alabama game (Bryant, 1974, p. 8).

Displaying the effect of Bryant's human resource behavior, Bob Gain, one of his players at Kentucky, said at a football reunion banquet several years after graduation, "I love you tonight for what I used to hate you for" (Bryant, 1974, p. 13). Bryant had a particularly soft spot for black players, the ones who would consistently "suck it up" and stick by him "because they didn't have anything to go back to" (Bryant, 1974, p. 17).

Bryant began to more fully appreciate and utilize human resource leadership behavior when he became an assistant to his college coach. Until he became an assistant, he hadn't realized that beneath all the outward toughness, he was just like most coaches who have a reputation for being tough—"he was a sentimental old man, just like me" (Bryant, 1974, p. 44). And to prove his point, he recalled a time when one of his star players, Babe Parilli, took a shot in the groin against North Texas State and needed an operation to relieve the pressure from internal bleeding. He went back to the college dormitory after the operation but got weaker. The next week, Bryant's wife, Mary Harmon, picked him up from the dormitory and brought him home to live with them.

His old rival, Bud Wilkinson from Oklahoma, showed him a classiness that he wished he himself had. Wilkinson came into the Alabama dressing room after they had beaten Oklahoma, ending their thirty-seven game winning streak, and shook hands with Bryant and as many of the players as he could reach. Bryant had never done that before, or seen it done. "But I've done it since," he said (Bryant, 1974, p. 104). For example, after a 7–6 loss to Georgia Tech, he went in the opposing team's locker room and called the captains out of the showers and shook hands with them. He congratulated Tech coach Bobby Dodd again, and when he was going back through the crowd, a woman who had a boy on Tech's team told him how proud she was. He said she had reason to be. Bryant was awfully satisfied with the way he had acted, saying, "Mama and Papa would have been proud of me" (Bryant, 1974, p. 187).

So, by the time he arrived at Alabama, Bryant displayed considerably more human resource behavior than he had in his previous head coaching stops at Kentucky and Texas A&M. On his first day at Alabama, he talked with each one of his players individually, asking them how they were doing in school, talking with them about their brothers and sisters, and in many cases visiting their homes to meet their parents.

However, much to his chagrin, he retained the reputation of being inordinately tough on his players. The logic of this attitude escaped Bryant. If he really taught brutality and treated people as badly as they claimed, how could he have recruited such great student athletes? According to Bryant, "The fact is that if I told Lee Roy Jordan or Steve Meilinger or John David Crow I needed them, they would start walking to Alabama right now" (Bryant, 1974, p. 180).

Finally, Bryant recalled a time after an Alabama loss when he cursed and otherwise berated his team on a very personal level. After thinking about it, he called a meeting to apologize to the squad; he told them that his language had demonstrated a lack of vocabulary on his part, that it showed weakness, and that from then on, every swear word he used on the practice field would cost him $10. By this time in his career, Coach Bryant had surely learned the value of appropriate human resource frame leadership behavior.

THE SYMBOLIC FRAME

In the symbolic frame, the organization is seen as a stage, a theater in which every actor plays certain roles, and the symbolic leader attempts to communicate the right impressions to the right audiences. Bear Bryant made extensive use of symbolic frame leadership behavior. Just the nickname "Bear" conjures up a certain image of toughness in most people's eyes. Hearing how he earned the nickname adds to that image. It seems that in his younger and less financially prosperous days, he was at a touring carnival with his friends when he encountered a sideshow that offered $1 a minute to anyone brave enough to get into a ring and fight a live bear. Paul Bryant did so and forever after was known as Bear Bryant. We don't know exactly how he fared in that ring, but we do know that he survived and that the carnival barker skipped town without paying Bryant his hard-earned money.

The manner in which Bear Bryant supervised his practices provides another instance of his use of symbolic leadership behavior. He was the first coach to use a tall tower that overlooked the practice field, projecting the "big brother" image that he intended. He stood up there wearing his signature houndstooth hat, looking for the first sign of lack of effort or loss of concentration on the part of his players and coaches. Once he saw something that he did not like, he said, "I would surprise myself at how quick I could get down from that tower at practice" (Bryant, 1974, p. 11). And, God help the offending person!

Once, when being interviewed by *Life* magazine, Bryant engaged in another instance of using symbolic frame behavior. He told the interviewer that his system was based on the "Ant Plan" and that he'd "gotten the idea watching a colony of ants in Africa during the war, a whole bunch of ants working toward a common goal" (Bryant, 1974, p. 140). The interviewer then asked him about his image as a strict disciplinarian. Bryant replied by telling the story of how his quarterback at Texas A&M, Roddy Osbourne, threw a late-game interception against Georgia Tech but was able to catch and tackle the player who intercepted the ball before he could score the winning touchdown. Everyone was wondering how the slow-footed Osbourne could catch a speed demon like the Georgia Tech defensive back. According to Bryant, "The difference was that the Georgia Tech kid was running for a touchdown and Osbourne was running for his life" (Bryant, 1974, p. 140).

Bryant was also fond of posting meaningful signs in the locker room as symbolic messages to his players. One of his favorites read, "Winning isn't everything, but it beats anything that comes in second." Another read, "Be good or be gone!" Still another cultivated his tough-guy image, reading, "To win, you have to out-mean people." Bryant also thought that the mere mention of Alabama football generated fear in the hearts of his opponents—and he did everything that he could to nurture that image. And in another display of symbolic leadership behavior, he initiated the "One Hundred Percent Club," which helped motivate his players to actualize their potential. Membership was based entirely on effort, not ability.

Bryant's pregame and halftime locker room speeches are legendary. In one case, when his team was going up against heavily favored Oklahoma, which was on an incredible three-year winning streak, he reminded his players of the parable of the mustard seed, where Jesus Christ told his disciples about how, even though the mustard seed was among the smallest in nature, it produced a large plant. Jesus said further that if a man had faith even as small as a mustard seed, he could move a mountain. Bryant applied the message of the mustard seed to this team and said that if they had faith in Alabama football, they would beat Oklahoma—and they did. In a bit of irony, however, when Bryant told his friend Bobby Dodd of Georgia Tech about his motivational mustard-seed speech, Dodd tried to use it before one of Tech's big games—and lost.

Bryant always had the symbolic tradition of praying before each game, but after an unbelievable last-second comeback against Rice University, his halfback, Lloyd Taylor, noted that they had prayed every time before a game, but afterward they didn't do anything. "What happened today, we didn't do. We got some help from upstairs. Let's pray." From then on, Bryant's teams prayed both before and after games.

Bryant also knew how to use symbolic behavior to counter some of the negative images that Alabama football had. For instance, in some quarters, Alabama had a poor academic image. In responding to a reporter who was insinuating that Joe Namath had majored in basket weaving at Alabama, Bryant responded that, in fact, Joe Namath did not major in basket weaving. "He majored in journalism. It was much easier" (Bryant, 1974, p. 201). Along these lines of overcoming the negative image that Alabama had, Bryant was particularly proud of a letter he received from Ara Parseghian shortly after Bryant's Alabama team defeated Notre Dame for the national championship. It was the only one he had ever received from a coach he had beaten, and it had said how much his team had enjoyed playing Alabama and how wrong their impressions had been beforehand.

Finally, Bryant used symbolic leadership behavior to further some of his ideals that transcended football. For example, when he was at the University of Kentucky, he convinced the president, Herman Donavan, that Kentucky should be the first university in the Southeastern Conference to have black players—and they were.

THE POLITICAL FRAME

Leaders operating out of the political frame clarify what they want and what they can get. Political leaders are realists above all. They never let what they want cloud their judgment about what is possible. They assess the distribution of power and interests. As I have pointed out before, virtually every coach has to behave in the political frame at some point is his or her career in order to be a truly effective leader. Much of the political frame behavior for coaches revolves around their own contract negotiations, as well as their relationships with their presidents, athletic directors, and star players. Accurately assessing the power distribution in these relationships will often determine whether the coach attains his or her ultimate goals.

Bear Bryant was very astute politically, but he learned to be so the hard way. When he was head coach at the University of Kentucky, no matter how successful he was, the basketball team under legendary coach Adolph Rupp was king. Bryant was a very proud man and took this as a personal affront. Reflecting back on his experience at Kentucky, Bryant observed that he had done some stupid things in his life. "I quit Kentucky because I got a mad on and made up my mind it just wasn't big enough for me and Adolph Rupp. Rupp and I should have complemented each other" (Bryant, 1974, p. 10). He further noted that he left Kentucky with nine years left on his contract. He left Texas A&M with seven years left, and Maryland with three left. "I've had seventy years of contracts in twenty-nine years of coaching" (Bryant, 1974, p. 66).

Bryant said that if he had it to do over again, he would reach out to Rupp and ask him to do something for him. Knowing how proud Rupp was, he would have been complimented by Bryant's asking him for advice or a favor. Bryant believed that if he had taken this politically savvy approach instead, he and Rupp would have become lifelong friends instead of mortal enemies.

In 1945, immediately before he went to Kentucky, Bryant had another negative encounter with the use of political frame behavior. That year Bryant accepted the job as head coach at the University of Maryland. In his only season with the Terrapins, Bryant led the team to a 6–2–1 record. However, there was a struggle for control of the football program between Bryant and Harry Clifton "Curley" Byrd. Byrd was a former Terrapin coach, and when Bryant was coach, he was the university president. In the most widely publicized example of a power struggle between the two strong-willed men, Bryant suspended a player for violating team rules only to discover that Byrd had the player reinstated while Bryant was away on vacation. As a result, Bryant left Maryland to take over the head coaching position at the University of Kentucky.

In a display of highly effective political frame behavior, Bryant was able to leverage his power at Texas A&M to have them place in his 1957 contract a percentage-of-the-gate clause, whereby he would receive a little over 1 percent of the gate receipts for home games for the remainder of his contract. "I don't think any coach ever got that kind of deal before or since" (Bryant, 1974, p. 157). Later in his career, he once again used his political clout to convince Joe Namath not to quit football and to fire his underworld friends from his Bachelors III nightclub. Once the NFL found out about his nightclub's connection with alleged mobsters, they threatened Namath with a suspension. The headstrong Namath refused to capitulate until he had his "talk" with Bryant.

Perhaps his most publicized use of political frame leadership behavior revolved around a *Saturday Evening Post* article by Furman Bisher that accused Bryant of advocating "brutal" football and allegedly "fixing" the outcome of the Alabama/Georgia game with Wally Butts, the former coach and current athletic director. With public opinion on his side, especially in the South, Bryant sued the *Saturday Evening Post* for $1 million and eventually won. As a result of losing its integrity, the *Saturday Evening Post* went out of business within two years.

CONCLUSION

Even though it can be argued that Bear Bryant primarily engaged in structural frame leadership behavior, it is very apparent that he also utilized a fair share of human resource, symbolic, and political leadership behavior. His teams were always well prepared and highly competitive, which is characteristic of a structural leader. Due to his use of human resource behavior, however, his players loved playing for him and remained loyal to him well after their football-playing days were over. As we have seen, his use of symbolic behavior, starting with his ever-present houndstooth hat to his peering down from his practice field tower, created and cultivated the distinct image of Bear Bryant and Alabama football. Finally, his astute use of political frame behavior enabled him to sustain his image, even under adverse conditions. Leaders and aspiring leaders can learn much by internalizing some of the leadership behavior modeled by Coach Bryant.

6

TONY DUNGY

If you want to lift yourself up, lift up someone else.

—Booker T. Washington

BACKGROUND

Born in 1955, Tony Dungy just recently retired as head coach of the Indianapolis Colts of the National Football League. He had been with the Colts since 2001, and became the first African American head coach to win the Super Bowl when his Colts defeated the Chicago Bears in 2007. Prior to that, between 1996 and 2001, he was the head coach of the Tampa Bay Buccaneers.

Dungy's parents were both educators. His father was a college professor, while his mother taught high school English. They encouraged their children to focus on academics. Dungy attended Parkside High School in Jackson, Michigan where he played on the basketball and football teams.

As a result of a successful high school career, Dungy was offered an athletic scholarship to the University of Minnesota and played for the Golden Gophers from 1973 to 1976. He started at quarterback in his freshman year and, after four years, finished as Minnesota's career leader in pass attempts, completions, touchdowns, and passing yardage. He received Minnesota's Most Valuable Player award twice.

After graduating from Minnesota, he was signed as a free agent by the Pittsburgh Steelers of the National Football League as a defensive back, a fate many African American quarterbacks in college football shared. He played as a special teams' player for the Steelers in 1977 and as defensive back on the Super Bowl champion 1978 team, leading the team in interceptions.

Dungy was traded to the San Francisco 49ers and retired the next year. Following his retirement, Dungy was invited to become an assistant coach for his alma mater, the University of Minnesota. After one season in charge of defensive backs, he was hired as an assistant coach with the Pittsburgh Steelers by Chuck Noll, who had coached him as a player. After eight years with the Steelers, he left Pittsburgh in 1989 to become the defensive backs coach for the Kansas City Chiefs, and took over the defensive coordinator position for the Minnesota Vikings in 1992. While at Minnesota, Dungy's defense was ranked first in the NFL.

As a result of his success as a defensive coordinator in Minnesota, Dungy achieved his dream of being an NFL head coach when he was named coach of the Tampa Bay Buccaneers in 1996. He began almost immediately to develop a winning program. In 1997, the Buccaneers finished second in the NFC Central Division, Tampa Bay's first winning season since 1982. Under Dungy, the Buccaneers made four play-off appearances and won their division in 1999. However, Tampa Bay struggled to reach the play-offs in his last four seasons. As a consequence, Dungy was fired in 2002. As fate would have it, the year following his firing, the Buccaneers easily defeated the Philadelphia Eagles in the 2002 NFC Championship game under Jon Gruden en route to the club's first Super Bowl victory.

Dungy became head coach of the Indianapolis Colts in 2002. The Colts were known for their potent offense under Payton Manning, and for their weak defense. Dungy began immediately to strengthen the Colts' defense. By the 2005 season, the Colts were widely expected to be a Super Bowl contender. The Colts won their first thirteen games, prompting much speculation about the possibility of their becoming the NFL's first team to finish the season undefeated since the Miami Dolphins in 1972. However, it was never to be and the Colts lost their fourteenth game of the year to the San Diego Chargers. The Colts did manage to obtain home-field advantage throughout the play-offs but were defeated in the divisional play-off round against the Pittsburgh Steelers and never made it to the Super Bowl.

However, in 2006, an improved Colt's team made a playoff run for the ages. They first defeated the Kansas City Chiefs, holding one of the NFL's best running backs to less than fifty yards. Next, they upset the heavily favored Baltimore Ravens in the divisional round. On January 21, 2007, the Colts defeated the New England Patriots to advance to the Super Bowl in the greatest comeback of all time in a conference title game. On February 4, 2007, Dungy's long-awaited dream finally came true, and he and his Indianapolis Colts won the Super Bowl.

Dungy is also well-known for his off-the-field work with charities. He has earned widespread respect both on and off the field due to what many see as his strong religious convictions and high personal standards for ethics and behavior, which inform his actions as both a coach and a member of his community. He has been active in many community-service organizations in the cities in which he has coached.

In Tampa Bay, he began a mentoring program for young people called Mentors for Life and provided Buccaneers' tickets for the participants. He also supported other charitable programs in the area, such a Big Brothers/Big Sisters, Boys & Girls Clubs of America, the Prison Crusade Ministries, foster-parenting organizations, and Family First. His community involvement continued in Indianapolis, where he helped launch the Basket of Hope program, which aids patients at the Riley Hospital for Children. In Indianapolis, he continued to assist Big Brothers/Big Sisters and the Boys & Girls Club in Indianapolis. He has indicated that he will remain committed to charitable causes during his retirement (Dungy, 2007; La Monte & Shook, 2004; Wikipedia.org).

SITUATIONAL LEADERSHIP ANALYSIS

Situational leadership models differ from the earlier trait and behavioral models in asserting that no single way of leading works for all situations.

Rather, appropriate behavior depends on the circumstances at a given time. Effective managers diagnose the situation, identify the leadership style or behavior that will be most effective, and then determine whether they can implement the required style.

Coach Dungy is a devotee of situational leadership theory. In numerous instances, he has expressed his view that effective leadership behavior changes depending on the situation. He reminds his assistant coaches of the situational nature of leadership behavior on a frequent basis. This view of leadership was passed on to him at an early age by his father, who was a college professor. His father believed that you cannot teach only one way with only one syllabus because while some students might get it, others will not. Students have different ways of learning and connecting, and Dungy believes that it's the teacher's job to make sure they are all doing so. In the same way, coaches must help players learn by communicating in a way that makes sense to each individual—and that means altering one's leadership behavior depending on the situation.

Dungy's parents always looked at every situation individually, regardless of what seemed fair to their children. "That's something that took me a while to appreciate," notes Dungy, "but learning to view each situation by itself has helped me in coaching" (Dungy, 2007, p. 19). He knows that he can have blanket rules, but blanket rules don't always fit every individual. "I need to treat everybody fairly, but fair doesn't always mean equal" (Dungy, 2007, p. 19). For example, a rookie might simply get an explanation from him if he has made a mistake, while a veteran making the same mistake might get "torched."

According to Dungy, who is a very religious person, the notion of treating different people in different ways is an outgrowth of the biblical teaching that "to whom much is given, much is required"—be it privileges, responsibilities, or material items. "And if God has given you a lot of ability, I believe you should be held to a higher level of expectation" (Dungy, 2007, p. 19).

In applying the situational approach, Dungy has learned that it doesn't matter how you win. You play to your team's strength, whether it's offense, defense, or special teams. And your strengths may vary depending on your personnel and the opposition's personnel in that particular game or that particular season. He believes the best way to achieve success in each of these three areas is through attention to detail and commitment to the fundamentals—that is, doing ordinary things better than anyone else. Suffice it to say, Tony Dungy sees the need to vary one's leadership behavior depending on the situation in order to maximize one's effectiveness. Just as effective teachers adapt their teaching style to the learning styles of their students, effective leaders need to modify and adapt their leadership style to the "readiness" level of their followers.

THE STRUCTURAL FRAME

Structural leaders seek to develop a new model of the relationship between structure, strategy, and environment in their organizations. Strategic planning, extensive preparation, and effecting change are priorities for them. In his balanced approach to leadership, Coach Dungy makes good use of structural frame leadership behavior when appropriate. Dungy was first made aware of the importance of structural behavior when he was an assistant to coach Chuck Noll of Pittsburgh Steelers fame. Coach Noll believed that champions don't beat themselves. In order to win, a team must do the ordinary things better than anyone else does—day in and day out. He did not believe in fooling other coaches or outscheming them. He wanted his teams to outplay them because they were better conditioned and better prepared. "When we get into a critical situation, we won't have to think. We'll play fast and fundamentally sound"—all notions of a structural leader and all notions that his pupil Dungy internalized (Dungy, 2007, p. 43).

In his first meeting with his teams, especially new teams, Dungy expresses his basic belief that champions are champions not because they do anything extraordinary but because they do the ordinary things better than anyone else. Thus, in this first meeting, he outlines four basic tenets that have become his coaching hallmarks:

1. Be in the top 5 in the NFL in give away/take away ratio.
2. Be in the top 5 in the NFL in fewest penalties.
3. Be in the top 5 in the NFL in overall special teams.
4. Make big plays; don't give up big plays.

Dungy applies these concepts not only to his own behavior but also to his hiring practices. Take his hiring of Herman Edwards: At first glance, Edwards and Dungy seem to be almost polar opposites. Edwards is emotional and talkative, while Dungy is more analytical and reserved. But that was exactly the type of person that Dungy wanted—someone to complement him. He wanted teachers more than tacticians, smart coaches who were driven to accomplish goals and could get these goals across. Together, they focused on fundamentals and making sure things were done the "right way."

Dungy places great emphasis on mastering the fundamentals of the game of football. Oftentimes, when things are not going well, coaches believe that they may have a faulty system. But Dungy believes that the best solution to poor play and falling just short of team goals is to focus on the fundamentals but perform them better. According to Dungy, if there was something wrong with the system, you would not have come so close in the first place.

In true structural leadership form, Dungy demands that his players be professional in their demeanor and act like champions. He expects them to respond to adversity without overreacting. They are to be on time: being late means that either something is not important to you or you can't be relied upon. He expects them to do what they are expected to do when they are expected to do it. Not almost; all the way. Not most of the time; all of the time. Take ownership! His motto is, "Whatever it takes. No excuses, and no explanations!" (Dungy, 2007, p. 116).

As we have seen, Dungy is a stickler for details. After a "blowup" at practice over some recalcitrance on the part of two of his players, Errict Rhett and Reggie Upshaw, the two players missed an appearance at a local school. Dungy was more angry over the missed session with the children than he was about what happened at practice. When the players took a cavalier attitude about missing the school appointment, Dungy reminded them in no uncertain terms that true champions know that it's *all* important. You have to understand that all the *little* things your coaches ask of you really do matter. He told them that knowing he could count on them was as important as their talent.

THE HUMAN RESOURCE FRAME

Human resource leaders believe in people and communicate that belief. They are passionate about *productivity through people*. Tony Dungy relies heavily on human resource behavior. We do not have to look far to find that Tony Dungy is basically a man with and for others. He is the epitome of the leader acting out of the human resource frame. That is not to say that he does not utilize the other three frames when appropriate, but he obviously feels comfortable behaving out of the human resource frame.

He learned the value of human resource leadership behavior by oftentimes being the object of a lack of human resource behavior. He remembers sweating out being cut by the Steelers at their summer training camp. He didn't know he had made the team until he saw his name above the locker. "I don't think Coach Chuck Noll even realized what an important lesson I learned that weekend" (Dungy, 2007, p. 45). It was an unforgettable and excruciating experience for Dungy. And to this day, he makes sure to tell his players how they are progressing and exactly when cuts are coming, and he gives them an hour-by-hour timetable for when they should turn on their cell phones and expect a call. And he does not assign the task to an assistant coach. He makes a point to make the calls himself and to meet with the players personally afterwards to explain his decision.

Dungy got what he considered a good piece of advice regarding the use of resource behavior from his friend, the great Pittsburgh Pirates baseball star Willie Stargell. Observing the tension in the locker room before the Buccaneers games, he noted that he had been playing baseball for a long time. When Stargell looked in Dungy's locker room before a game, he could not believe how tight everybody was. As for him, he always heard the umpire say, "Play ball!" He never once heard him say, "Work ball!" He told Dungy that having fun was something that football guys had forgotten. Dungy filed that away, not realizing how often he would draw on that thought later when he had to prepare his teams for big games.

He put what he had learned about the need for human resource behavior to use early on when he became head coach of the Tampa Bay Buccaneers. As soon as he arrived in Tampa, he began meeting with the players who lived there, trying to understand from them what needed to be fixed. One of the first moves he made was to put an end to the hazing of rookies during training camp. He didn't see the worth of it and much preferred more humane ways of cultivating the sense of trust and togetherness that would be crucial to his team down the road.

Many of his football-coaching brethren advised him to make the players afraid of him—afraid of being cut, afraid of being benched. But Dungy did not believe in that approach. He has always believed that if you tell people what needs to be done, they will do it—if they have confidence in you and believe that your motives are altruistic. He believes that people see through manipulation and exploitation but will respond to those leaders whom they believe really care about them. He had grown up with this philosophy, which his mentor, Chuck Noll, reinforced later in life. His mother used to tell him that people follow a good leader because they want to, not because he makes them.

Dungy wants his organization to emphasize character, values, and family, and he wants it to extend out to the community. He models this behavior, treating everyone with dignity and spending many hours on community service. As noted earlier, he began a mentoring program for young people called Mentors for Life and provided Buccaneers tickets for the participants. He also supported other charitable programs. In Indianapolis, he helped launch the Basket of Hope program, which aids patients at the Riley Hospital for Children.

Dungy really wants to show people that you can win "all kinds of ways." He says that he coaches the way he wanted to be coached. He believes that he has lost a couple of job opportunities because his style goes against the grain, against the culture. The conventional wisdom in football is that "nice guys finish last." For your faith to be more important than your job, for your family to be more important than your job—this is anathema to many football people. But Dungy proved that a human resource approach could work.

Sometimes advice on the use of human resource behavior comes from unexpected sources. Indianapolis Colts placekicker Mike Vanderjagt once complained to the press that the Colts needed somebody who was going to "get in people's faces and yell and scream" (Dungy, 2007, p. 215). He believed that Dungy was too mild mannered and even-keeled to succeed. Dungy's first instinct upon hearing of this outburst was to respond in kind by cutting Vanderjagt. But his young son, Jamie, convinced him to "play it cool." The next day, Vanderjagt publicly apologized for his untimely outburst and, as a result, was kept on the team. Dungy used Matthew 21:28–32 to justify his approach. This Bible verse refers to Jesus's parable about the father who sent his two sons to work in the vineyard. The first son at first refused but, after further thought, went into the vineyard to work. The second son agreed to work in the vineyard but never went. Vanderjagt was like the first son, according to Dungy. "What is in your heart is important; not words" (Dungy, 2007, p. 215).

THE SYMBOLIC FRAME

In the symbolic frame, the organization is seen as a stage, a theater in which every actor plays certain roles, and the symbolic leader attempts to communicate the right impressions to the right audiences. Tony Dungy makes thoughtful and extensive use of symbolic frame leadership behavior. For example, one of Dungy's strong tendencies is to utilize epitaphs and other inspirational pieces in the locker room and elsewhere, like the one with which we began this chapter: if you want to lift yourself up, lift up someone else. Another of his favorites is a quote from Ralph Waldo Emerson: "Do not go where the path may lead; go instead to where there is no path and leave a trail" (Dungy, 2007, p. xi). Placing some of these values into action, Dungy puts the team owners and assistant coaches in first class on team flights, while he sits in coach with the players.

Dungy often uses symbolic behavior when he is being interviewed. For example, after hearing his locker room comments after the Super Bowl, a fan e-mailed the following: "My son and I watched your comments after the game together. I could take him to church twenty times, and it wouldn't have opened up a chance for us to talk the way watching the Super Bowl did" (Dungy, 2007, p. xii). Commenting on his own personal philosophy, Dungy has said, "It's the journey that matters. Learning is more important than the test. Practice well, and the games will take care of themselves" (Dungy, 2007, p. xiv). In this light, he continually preaches to his teams that he expects them to live and play by the concept "whatever it takes," adding a second phrase: "No excuses, no explanations" (Dungy, 2007, p. 106).

When he first came to Tampa Bay, Dungy engaged in some symbolic behavior to offset the previous ownership's image of excessive frugality by replacing the college dormitory housing at the training-camp facility with downtown hotels like the Marriott, the Wyndham, and the Ritz-Carlton. He saw this as a small change that would ready his players for the bigger changes he would later demand of them. At first, he tried to change the location of the training camp because he felt that the players associated it with losing. However, there just wasn't enough money in the budget to do so. Nevertheless, he changed the lax routine and created a Spartan atmosphere as a symbol for wanting his team to be mentally and physically tougher.

Although football has been a big and enjoyable part of his life, he views it as a means to do something more—to share his faith, to encourage and lift up others—and he takes advantage of the platform that it has provided. For example, he chose not to use profanity because of his religious faith. He never mandated that approach for anyone else. He simply asked his players and coaches to be mindful of their language when they had open practices during training camp and to lead by example. Again, because of his strong religious beliefs, Dungy often expresses himself in biblical terms. The year after he was fired by the Bucs, they went on to win the Super Bowl under his successor, Jon Gruden. Dungy responded in typical symbolic leadership fashion by saying that he now knew what Moses must have felt. He had led the Israelites for forty years through the desert, but he was not allowed to enter the Promised Land.

In encouraging his Indianapolis Colts to get to the Super Bowl after a number of "just misses," Dungy used the "death by inches" imagery he had seen in Frank Sinatra's performance in the movie *Von Ryan's Express*. While fleeing the Nazis, Sinatra's character runs to jump onto a moving train and is inches short of grabbing the hand of a fellow prisoner to be pulled onto the train. Dungy said that if his team just focused more on the details, the inches, they could reach their goal of getting to the Super Bowl rather than coming up just inches short.

So that his players are always thinking ahead, Dungy has established the tradition of distributing a vision document to them before the last game of the year. It varies somewhat from year to year, but the essential message remains the same: The first step toward creating an improved future is developing the ability to envision it. Vision will ignite the fire of passion that fuels one's commitment to do "whatever it takes" to achieve excellence. Only vision allows one to transform dreams of greatness into the reality of achievement through human action. Vision has no boundaries and knows no limits. "Our vision is what we become in life," writes Dungy (Dungy, 2007, p. 125).

Like every effective symbolic leader, Dungy has modeled the behavior that he expects in his followers. He began a mentoring program for young people called Mentor for Life and also supports other charitable programs, like Big Brothers/Big Sisters, Boys & Girls Club of America, and the Prison Crusade Ministries. In the summer of 1998, Family

First launched a new program called All Pro Dad. Dungy hosted an event where fathers brought their children and interacted with them at football camp. This is just a small sampling of his involvement with charitable organizations.

As mentioned earlier, Dungy is a religious man and often uses religious imagery to get his points across. For example, he believes that we are all part of God's grand plan and that we should place ourselves in his hands. He often refers to the story of Joseph, the father of Jesus, and how Joseph surrendered himself to the will of God, knowing that God works for our good—"whether we can see it now or not" (Dungy, 2007, p. 198). Because of his strong religious convictions, Dungy often speaks out against what he perceives to be immoral or unethical behavior. For example, he spoke out against a sexually suggestive commercial featuring football star Terrell Owens and an actress from the television show *Desperate House Wives*. The actress steps out of a shower in the football locker room dressed only in a towel, suggesting that Owens forget about the football game and accompany her to her room instead. Aired during Monday Night Football, the ad, Dungy believed, sent the wrong message about morality, responsibility, and NFL players to kids. In still another reference to his religious beliefs, Dungy reacted to his son's suicide by reminding us that "God can provide joy in the midst of a sad occasion. Our challenge today is to *find* that joy" (Dungy, 2007, p. 250). Finally, in motivating his team for an upcoming play-off game against the New England Patriots, he used the Bible story of David and Goliath to inspire them. He urged his team to look at New England the way that David looked at Goliath—not as a giant but as just another adversary. He also pointed out that King Saul offered David armor, but he turned it down in favor of his usual slingshot; the Colts, therefore, should do nothing different for the New England game. And when Goliath fell, David took no chances and cut the giant's head off; if the Colts got ahead in the game, Dungy wanted his team to "bury them" (Dungy, 2007, p. 282).

Dungy once used the image of McDonald's to get a point across to his team. He believed that one reason for his team's difficulty in getting to the Super Bowl was a lack of consistency. According to Dungy, the beauty of McDonald's is its consistency. When you order a McDonald's cheeseburger and fries, no matter where you are in the world when you do so, you know exactly what to expect. That was the kind of consistency that he wanted from his team, week in and week out. By the way, he got the McDonald's idea from his kids.

Lastly, Dungy also used symbolic behavior in communicating the team rules to his players. Instead of simply telling them his expectations or posting them on a bulletin board, he used creativity and distributed his "Five Things That May Get You in *USA Today*" list:

1. Alcohol or illegal drugs
2. Being out after 1 a.m.
3. Driving more than 20 mph over the speed limit
4. Guns
5. Women you don't know well enough or whom you know too well (Dungy, 2007, p. 272)

THE POLITICAL FRAME

Leaders operating out of the political frame clarify what they want and what they can get. Political leaders are realists above all. They never let what they want cloud their judgment about what is possible. They assess the distribution of power and interests. As with virtually all of his coaching counterparts, Tony Dungy has had occasion to utilize political leadership behavior. For example, in dealing with the media, he advises his players to be eternally aware of their presence and not to do anything that will bring on their wrath. Don't think if you treat them rudely, they will suddenly disappear. In fact, "they'll just make life more miserable" (Dungy, 2007, p. 113). So, he advises his players to do anything that they can to pacify the media and to avoid giving them a reason for rancor. In his own dealings with the media, Dungy models this behavior.

In another display of political frame behavior, Dungy threatened to pull his team off the field when Carolina Jaguars owner Wayne Weaver tried to enforce his club policy of not allowing children on the sideline during games. Dungy encouraged the primacy of family with his players and urged them to join him in having their sons and daughters with them on the sidelines from time to time. When Weaver tried to enforce his policy, Dungy reminded him of how much revenue he would be losing if he had to refund the ticket price to sixty thousand fans if Dungy were to pull his team off the field. Needless to say, Weaver capitulated.

In another instance, the Tampa Buccaneer ownership wanted to fire Mike Shula, Dungy's offensive coordinator. Dungy had second thoughts because he did not believe that Shula bore sole responsibility for the Bucs' trouble scoring, but he reluctantly agreed. A few days later, however, he changed his mind. He just could not allow the injustice to take place. When Mike Shula learned that his presence could ultimately place Dungy's job in jeopardy, he voluntarily resigned. Looking back, Dungy believes that this situation was the first chink in the Bucs' armor that weakened staff unity. The decision turned out to be the one that Dungy "most regretted in [his] coaching career" (Dungy, 2007, p. 168).

CONCLUSION

Tony Dungy could be a poster child for the appropriate use of situational leadership theory. He is a master at balancing all four leadership frames in his overall leadership behavior. He understands the need for thorough preparation and planning if one wishes to be successful (structural frame). The title of one of his books is *Quiet Strength*, which indicates the value that he attaches to human resource leadership behavior. His use of symbolic frame leadership behavior is extensive and permeating. While he uses political frame leadership behavior sparingly, all indications are that he does so appropriately. Leaders and aspiring leaders have much to learn from observing and reflecting upon Tony Dungy's leadership style.

7

JOE GIBBS

Life is a series of fourth and ones.

—Joe Gibbs

BACKGROUND

Born in 1940, Joe Gibbs is a member of both the football and the NAS-CAR Hall of Fame. Most recently, he coached the Washington Redskins, serving his second term with the team. He retired from coaching for the second time at the end of the 2007 season.

Gibbs is well-known for his work ethic, and had been successful by simply outworking his coaching counterparts. During his first stint in the National Football League, he coached the Washington Redskins for twelve seasons and led them to an astounding eight play-off appearances and three Super Bowl titles. After retiring for the first time after the 1992 season, he switched focus to his NASCAR team, Joe Gibbs Racing, which won three championships under his ownership. In 2004, Gibbs was coaxed out of retirement to rejoin the Redskins as head coach and team president.

Gibbs graduated from Santa Fe High School in California in 1959, where he was the star quarterback. He attended Cerritos Junior College and San Diego State University, where he played tight end, offensive guard, and linebacker. San Diego State University was then coached by Don Coryell, who later became a very successful NFL coach. Gibbs gained much knowledge about the passing game from Coryell. Gibbs graduated from San Diego State in 1964 and earned a master's degree in 1966, making him, along with Bill Walsh, the coaches with the most formal education among those profiled in this book.

After graduation, Gibbs began his coaching career as an offensive line coach at San Diego State. He then moved to Florida State before serving under John McKay, another future NFL coach at Southern California and Frank Broyles at Arkansas. His former college coach, Don Coryell, brought Gibbs to the National Football League as the offensive backfield coach for the St. Louis Cardinals. After a season as offensive coordinator for the Tampa Bay Buccaneers under John McKay, Gibbs rejoined Coryell who was now with the San Diego Chargers.

While at San Diego, Gibbs coordinated the highly successful "Air Coryell" offense. Using a sophisticated passing attack, the Chargers with quarterback Dan Fouts set a number of offensive records during Gibbs's two seasons there. Finally, after seventeen years of coaching as an assistant, Gibbs was offered a job as the head coach of the Washington Redskins by legendary owner Jack Kent Cooke.

In his first season with the Redskins the team lost its first five games. Jack Kent Cooke publicly expressed confidence in Gibbs, predicting that the team would finish 8–8. The newly inspired team improved immensely and ended the season with an 8–8 record just as Cooke predicted. In only his second season with the Redskins, one shortened by strikes, Gibbs led the team to an NFC Championship, and a Super Bowl victory.

The next season saw Gibbs's surprising success continue, and the Redskins once again advanced to the Super Bowl. Although the Redskins were an overwhelming favorite going into the game, they were soundly defeated by the Los Angeles Raiders. Three years later, in 1986, Gibbs coached the team back to the NFC Championship game but lost to the New York Giants. The following season, the Redskins got into the play-offs and reached the Super Bowl, where they rode to victory on the arm of quarterback Doug Williams, the first black quarterback to win a Super bowl, to defeat the Denver Broncos.

In 1991, the Redskins cruised through the play-offs to the Super Bowl, thus giving Gibbs his third and final Super Bowl title. The next year, the Redskins were not successful in defending their Super Bowl crown and lost early in the play-offs. Gibbs suddenly retired in early 1993, citing health problems, and a desire to spend more time with his family.

In 1996, Gibbs was enshrined in the Pro Football Hall of Fame. At the time, his combined winning percentage of .683 was third all-time behind Vice Lombardi and John Madden. Gibbs is also the only NFL coach to ever win three Super Bowls with three different quarterbacks and three different starting running backs.

Throughout his retirement, many NFL owners approached him, hoping to lure him back to coaching, but to no avail. Finally, after spending eleven years in retirement from the NFL, Gibbs was successfully lured out of retirement in 2003 by Daniel Snyder, the new Redskin's owner.

His second NFL tour of duty paled in comparison to his first. In 2004, Gibbs had what was, up to that point, the worst season of his career with a 6–10 record. Critics questioned whether the game had passed him by. However, in 2005, Gibbs led his team to a 10–6 record. This earned the Redskins their first play-off berth since 1999. After completing the 2007 regular season, the Redskins had a record of nine wins and seven losses. They advanced as the wild card team in the NFC; however, they were defeated by the Seattle Seahawks in the first round of the play-offs. Gibbs retired after the 2007 season for the second time (Gibbs & Jenkins, 1991; Gibbs & Abraham, 2003; Wikipedia.org).

SITUATIONAL LEADERSHIP ANALYSIS

Situational leadership models differ from the earlier trait and behavioral models in asserting that no single way of leading works in all situations. Rather, appropriate behavior depends on the circumstances at a given time. Effective managers diagnose the situation, identify the leadership style or behavior that will be most effective, and then determine whether they can implement the required style.

The mere fact that Joe Gibbs was the only coach to win three Super Bowls with three different quarterbacks gives testament to the fact that he is quite able to adapt his leadership behavior to the situation. Those three quarterbacks, Joe Theismann, Doug Williams, and Mark Rypien, had very different skills and personalities. Nevertheless, Gibbs was able to adapt his leadership behavior in such a way as to maximize each of their capabilities and strengths.

However, like many leaders, he learned of the need to adapt one's leadership behavior to the situation the hard way. When he first became coach of the Washington Redskins, he thought that he could simply use the same system with which he was successful at San Diego. Consequently, the Redskins started the season 0–6. Gibbs had hoped to fit Redskin personnel into what had worked for him at San Diego, and by the time he realized he had made a mistake, it was too late. He decided right then that he had to adapt his leadership behavior to the current situation and immediately "started tinkering with things" (Gibbs & Jenkins, 1991, p. 119). It was also then that the Redskins went on a winning streak and ended that season 8–8. From that moment on, Gibbs was careful to adjust his leadership behavior to whatever was appropriate in a given situation and not to be locked into one way, and only one way, of doing things.

THE STRUCTURAL FRAME

Structural leaders seek to develop a new model of the relationship between structure, strategy, and environment in their organizations. Strategic planning, extensive preparation, and effecting change are priorities for them. The conventional belief is that Joe Gibbs was basically a structural leader. There is much evidence to support this belief.

As with many structural leaders, Joe Gibbs was an avowed workaholic. He was a good athlete in his youth because he worked hard at it. He did not have natural ability, great speed, or agility. He became a good athlete through hard work, and he believed that he would become an excellent coach the same way. Gibbs also believed that a by-product of his lack of natural ability was his fierce competitiveness.

However, he also came to learn that he should not depend entirely on one frame of leadership behavior. His experience playing and coaching with Don Coryell had a great impact on him. Don Coryell was progressive and liberal. Gibbs felt that the contrast in styles was great for him. "I tended to be rigid," he claimed. "For me everything had to be perfect. For Don, looseness and flexibility were okay" (Gibbs & Jenkins, 1991, p. 69).

In true structural leadership fashion, Gibbs was confident of his abilities. He was optimistic that he would be successful in his first head coaching assignment because he had been preparing for it his whole life. He had plenty of ideas. He had learned how to run an offense. He knew what he wanted to see on defense, in the training room, and on the practice field. He also knew what kind of men he wanted to assist him. In short, he had a plan. Even in his first year with the Redskins, when he was struggling to keep his head above water, he found a way to motivate both himself and his players. There would be no play-offs that year, no glory, but they wanted that last win. "We were playing for respect, for ourselves, and for the fans" (Gibbs & Jenkins, 1991, p. 130).

Indicative of his tendency toward structural leadership behavior was Gibbs's fond telling of the story of the coach who had just lost a heart-breaking game by one point on a missed extra point. When he arrived home, his wife tried to place things in perspective and said, "You've still got me and the kids, and we have this lovely home." To which the coach responded, "Yeah, and I'd trade all of it for one extra point" (Gibbs & Jenkins, 1991, p. 123).

In contrast to this extreme structural frame attitude, however, Gibbs knew that in order to be most effective, he had to "sprinkle" in a little human resource behavior to keep things in perspective. At a particularly stressful time during one game, Gibbs noticed his young son, Coy, quietly playing with his trucks on the Redskins sideline, totally oblivious of his father's turmoil. It made him wonder which was the true perspective? "We get so caught up in the externals of life, and we run the risk of losing the things most important to us, our own kids," he said (Gibbs & Jenkins, 1991, p. 173).

Nevertheless, during the season, he was immersed in football. It commanded almost every waking minute, and he could be bothered with nothing else. He believed that there was no other way to function as a coach in the NFL. And in true structural frame fashion, Gibbs believed that to win it all, "a team has to be obsessive about the fundamentals and the little things" (Gibbs & Jenkins, 1991, p. 238). Even during the NFL Players

Union strike, he told the replacement players that they were expected to play to win, not just to keep the cash flowing. He let them know immediately that "this was serious business" (Gibbs & Jenkins, 1991, p. 238).

Gibbs took responsibility for planning. He worked hard to analyze every game and prepare for the next one. He demanded that his team stay in shape, master the offenses and defenses, and learn to play together. He believed that the three keys to winning are the game plan, conditioning, and motivation. He expected peak performances from himself, his staff, and his players. "Sometimes we lose anyway," he said, but he never accepted losing (Gibbs & Jenkins, 1991, p. 264). He picked the loss apart and couldn't wait until he faced that same team again. Even when the other team was clearly better and better coached, he dwelled on the loss until he figured it out. According to Gibbs's structural mind set, "Maybe winning isn't everything or the only thing, but it sure is the object of the game" (Gibbs & Jenkins, 1991, p. 264).

Gibbs even took on religion in his predisposition toward the structural frame of leadership. Being a deeply religious man himself, Gibbs was critical of football players who believe in Christ and think that means they should be softer and less aggressive. He believed they were wrong and did not take the profession seriously enough. The believers had more reason than anyone to be the best, he believed. Football is an aggressive game, and some of the most aggressive people he had met were Christian football players, such as Reggie White, an ordained minister. According to Gibbs, "If you've been given a gift, whether as a player or a coach, you have an obligation to make the absolute most of that" (Gibbs & Jenkins, 1991, p. 278).

THE HUMAN RESOURCE FRAME

Human resource leaders believe in people and communicate that belief. They are passionate about *productivity through people*. The human resource frame is another leadership frame in which Joe Gibbs feels comfortable. There is abundant evidence that he sees the value of appropriately applied human resource leadership behavior.

Gibbs observed the effectiveness of appropriately applied human resource leadership behavior through his friend and former great NFL receiver, Raymond Berry. When both Gibbs and Berry were assistant coaches at Arkansas, Gibbs saw how Berry was better able than he to convince recruits to come to Arkansas through his effective use of human resource behavior. Gibbs was deeply influenced by Berry, who had such a peace about him that he commanded respect. He was soft-spoken, and the players listened to his every word. By his own admission, unlike his friend Raymond Berry, Gibbs at this stage of his career was an egotist. He wanted things his way and did not have much time for people who disagreed with him. However, he learned from Berry that the appropriate use of human resource behavior can go a long way in making one a more effective leader.

Once he learned the value of human resource frame leadership behavior, Gibbs utilized it to his advantage. Upon accepting the position to coach the Redskins, one of his first challenges was to try to resign star running back John Riggins, who had sat out the entire previous year in a contract dispute. Until then, the Redskins had taken a very structural frame approach and "waited Riggins out." Gibbs saw the futility of that approach: Riggins was so stubborn that he would never have capitulated. So, Gibbs decided to apply some human resource behavior to this unique situation. Without saying anything to anybody, he got on a plane and flew to Lawrence, Kansas, where Riggins lived. He waited overnight for an "audience" with the proud football star. Riggins arrived at the meeting in fatigues and drinking a beer. Gibbs overlooked his appearance and treated him with deference and respect. Riggins reacted by saying, "I'll tell you what. If you get me back, I'll make you famous" (Gibbs & Jenkins, 1991, p. 115). He came back, and by Gibbs own account, he made Gibbs famous.

Gibbs earned the trust and respect of his players because they came to know that he really cared for them. In fact, when he was named Coach of the Year after his first Super Bowl victory, he was just as happy for Mark Moseley, his placekicker, who was named Most Valuable Player and the five Redskins who were named to the Pro Bowl. He also showed his concern for his players by taking it upon himself to tell them personally when they were cut from the squad. He refused to delegate that responsibility, as most of his football coaching counterparts did. Gibbs also displayed this concern for other people's welfare in his business activities. During the off-season, he was involved in a real estate venture that went bankrupt. He insisted on facing every one of the bankers involved and telling them the truth. He told them exactly what had happened and exactly what he had to do with it. He vowed to work something out whereby he could repay his debts and not take the easy road of declaring bankruptcy.

When the press was becoming critical of Joe Theismann toward the end of his career, Gibbs defended him. "It was as if all those years and all those gutsy plays and all that loyalty and productivity had made him part of me" (Gibbs & Jenkins, 1991, p. 226). Gibbs could see things through Theismann's eyes. The poor passes and the blown plays were not entirely his fault, as the press insisted. In Gibbs eyes, he was still the Theismann of old. However, Gibbs later made a mistake with regard to the appropriate use of human resource behavior that ended up haunting him. When Theismann broke his leg severely, an injury that would ultimately end his career, Gibbs failed to visit him in the hospital. Gibbs rationalized his actions by claiming that he was deeply involved in game planning for an upcoming play-off game. The fact of the matter, however, was that Joe Gibbs had decided that structural behavior was more important at that moment than human resource behavior. Theismann reacted by saying, "One thing I need to tell you, Coach, is that you should have come to see me in the hospital." Despite their closeness, Theismann never truly forgave Gibbs for this perceived slight.

Gibbs even made room for the use of human resource behavior with the replacement players that he coached during the strike year. His regulars knew him well enough to know what he thought of them. He hated to see anything hurt them or their families or their futures. However, he was excited about coaching and winning with the young replacement players, and he treated them with as much care and respect as he did his regulars.

THE SYMBOLIC FRAME

In the symbolic frame, the organization is seen as a stage, a theater in which every actor plays certain roles, and the symbolic leader attempts to communicate the right impressions to the right audiences. Much of Joe Gibbs' use of symbolic leadership behavior revolved around his strong religious convictions and his reputation for being an acknowledged "student of the game." He was considered by many to be the intellectual type, although he challenged that assumption. "Maybe it's the glasses," he said. "I'm basically a physical guy, not a reader" (Gibbs & Jenkins, 1991, p. 25). Still, the image endured.

Gibbs admitted to being a very religious man and applying religious principles to his personal and professional lives. In church Gibbs learned that God made us and that he made us special. He believed that God, not some inert force, had created the world. "It just made sense," he said (Gibbs & Jenkins, 1991, p. 27). He believed that the Bible, even the Old Testament, applies to individuals today. While going through both personal and professional crises, Gibbs searched out passages in the Bible to guide him through. In effect, he wore his religious beliefs on his coat sleeve and modeled what he perceived to be desired behavior.

As he saw it, no one could have made so many career moves, traveling all over the country in pursuit of a career in the NFL, and have it turn out so perfectly without the help of Divine Providence. For instance, Gibbs recalled a time when his Redskins were about to play the mighty Miami Dolphins in the Super Bowl. He turned to his Bible, which just happened to open to the page that described the story of David and Goliath. Why should he be afraid of a new experience? Why should he be afraid of even the mighty Miami Dolphins? "If I belong to God, and David can kill Goliath, who knows? Maybe even the Redskins can best the Dolphins," he asserted (Gibbs & Jenkins, 1991, p. 148).

He realized that in life it was always fourth and one, and there were always people urging him not to play it safe and to go for it. But he always relied on his "gut feeling in both his personal and professional life," believing that he was in some way being guided by the hand of God. Along these lines, he got involved in charitable causes, like ministering to troubled teenagers, in every city in which he lived. He did so again when he arrived in Washington, D.C., modeling his program after that of Olympic weightlifter Paul Anderson in Dallas. Roger Stauback and Tom Landry helped Gibbs in Washington, and together they raised over $1 million per year for the troubled teenagers in that city.

Gibbs felt a moral obligation to use the platform that his job had given him to share with others what he thought was most important in life—and it wasn't football. He considered football a means to an end. He still hated losing, but he believed that although football has many qualities, it is not eternal. It is not about God and what he should mean to us. To make his point, Gibbs uses the Bible quote, "What does it profit a man to gain the whole world and lose his soul?"

None of these beliefs, however, impacts the basic nature of football. It is a very physical sport, and success requires aggressive behavior on the field. Gibbs did not allow his religious convictions to affect that part of the game. In fact, he was not at all shocked when he boarded the team bus at Redskin Park to head to the airport for a Dallas game and found his team members all dressed in battle fatigues—although, in this case, it might have been the "battle fire with fire" Bible passage that was at work.

THE POLITICAL FRAME

Leaders operating out of the political frame clarify what they want and what they can get. Political leaders are realists above all. They never let what they want cloud their judgment about what is possible. They assess the distribution of power and interests. There is evidence that Joe Gibbs used political frame leadership behavior when appropriate. For example, during the strike year (1982), he had to balance his support for the regular players and his responsibility to his owner and the replacement players to field a competitive team. He had always been "pro-player," but he had to face the fact that he was management. At the same time, he knew that his regulars would eventually return, and he wanted the team chemistry that they had developed to remain intact. In a prototypical display of political leadership behavior, Gibbs was so successful at bridging these two sets of conflicting responsibilities that his team ultimately won its first Super Bowl that year.

CONCLUSION

Although the evidence seems to indicate that Joe Gibbs felt most comfortable in the structural frame, in many instances he adapted his leadership behavior to the situation and appropriately practiced the other three frames of leadership behavior. His teams were reputedly well prepared and well conditioned, demonstrating his use of structural frame behavior. He was also known as a "players' coach" because of how effectively he related to his players, which is indicative of human resource frame leadership behavior. His use of symbolic frame leadership behavior in operationalizing his religious convictions is legendary, and his use of political frame leadership behavior was evident during the 1982 players' strike and in his stellar relationship with upper management. In summary, Joe Gibbs modeled an exemplary ability to adapt his leadership behavior to the situation.

BILL PARCELLS

Show me a good loser, and I'll show you a loser.

—Red Auerbach

BACKGROUND

Born in 1941, in Englewood, New Jersey, Bill Parcells is currently executive vice president of football operations for the Miami Dolphins of the National Football League, but has made his reputation as a football coach, having coached a number of teams, most recently the Dallas Cowboys. He is known as the "Big Tuna," a nickname derived from the "Charlie Tuna" character on a popular brand of canned tuna fish. He earned two Super Bowl rings as coach of the New York Giants.

Parcells played high school football at River Dell Regional High School in New Jersey. He was recruited as a linebacker by Wichita State University. Before entering the professional ranks, he held positions at the collegiate level at Hastings, Wichita State, Army, Florida State, Vanderbilt, and Texas Tech. He was also the head coach at the Air Force Academy.

Parcells began his professional career in 1979 with the New York Giants as the defensive coordinator under Ray Perkins. It was with the New York Giants that he first became acquainted with another coach profiled in this study, Bill Belechick. He ultimately became Belechick's champion and mentor. In 1980, he left New York to join the New England Patriots as the linebackers coach for one year before returning to the Giants as defensive coordinator and linebackers coach. When Perkins left the Giants at the end of the season to become head coach at the University of Alabama, Parcells was named his successor.

When Parcells took over in 1983, the New York Giants had posted just one winning season in the previous ten years. His first year was no exception. He made a controversial decision to bench Phil Simms in favor of Scott Brunner, which resulted in a disastrous 3–12–1 season. After a disappointing first season, Parcells made Simms the starter again. The following year the team's record improved to 9–7. The next year the Giants were 10–6, earning them their first back-to-back play-off appearances in thirty years. In 1986, Parcells led the Giants to the first of two Super Bowls. In 1986, the Giants compiled a franchise best 14–2 record. Parcells's stifling 3–4 defense led by Lawrence Taylor, Carl Banks, Harry Carson, and Leonard Marshall, together with an offense under the direction of Phil Simms, routed the Denver Broncos 39–20 in the Super Bowl.

Three years later, Parcells led the Giants to a second Super Bowl. The Giants began the 1990 season 10–0, but lost Phil Simms to injury late in the season. Playing with a backup quarterback in Jeff Hostetler, the Giants still prevailed and beat the New England Patriots to win their second Super Bowl under Parcells. Parcells retired from football for the first of three times after the Super Bowl victory citing health problems.

Parcells then spent time as a football analyst for NBC Sports from 1991 to 1992. But after a two-year hiatus, Parcells returned to the NFL in 1993 as the head coach for the New England Patriots. Almost immediately, he molded the Patriots into a contender. In 1996, he led the Patriots to the Super Bowl but lost to the Green Bay Packers. Parcells left the Patriots over span-of-control issues.

The New York Jets were extremely interested in hiring Parcells as their coach to replace the ineffective Rich Kotite. However his contract did not allow him to coach elsewhere. As noted in Chapter 3, in order to circumvent Parcells's contractual obligations, the Jets hired Bill Belichick, Parcells's assistant, as the team's coach, then hired Parcells in an "advisory" capacity. New England threatened legal action against Parcells and the Jets. Then, New England appealed to NFL Commissioner, Paul Tagliabue, who brokered a deal between the two teams, with New England releasing Parcells from his contract and the Jets giving New England a first-round draft choice.

In his first year with the Jets, Parcells orchestrated a remarkable turnaround, leading the Jets to a 9–7 record. In 1998, the Jets went to the play-offs with a 12–4 record but lost to the eventual Super Bowl-champion Denver Broncos in the AFC Championship game. In 1999, quarterback Vinny Testaverde ruptured his Achilles tendon and the Jets finished 8–8. After the season, Bill Parcells retired from football for the second time, but remained with the Jets as their general manager.

Four years later, the Dallas Cowboys lured Bill Parcells out of retirement and made him their head coach in 2003. In his first season with the Cowboys, he led them to the play-offs with a 10–6 record, becoming the first head coach in NFL history to guide four different teams to the play-offs.

Following a couple of relatively successful years, Parcells finished his stay with Dallas with a 34–32 record and no play-off wins. He once again announced his retirement from football coaching in January 2007. On December 19, 2007, the *Miami Herald* reported that Parcells had agreed to become the new executive vice president of football operations for the Miami Dolphins, a position he still holds (Gutman, 2000; Parcells, 1987; Parcells & Coplon, 1995; Wikipedia.org).

SITUATIONAL LEADERSHIP ANALYSIS

Situational leadership models differ from the earlier trait and behavioral models in asserting that no single way of leading works in all situations. Rather, appropriate behavior depends on the circumstances at a given time. Effective managers diagnose the situation, identify the leadership style or behavior that will be most effective, and then determine whether they can implement the required style.

Whether instinctively or consciously, Bill Parcells understood the
need to vary one's leadership behavior, depending on the situation, from
the earliest moments of his coaching career. Parcells is a man of many
faces. He can charm you with an unexpectedly broad smile or destroy
you with a withering glance that can make even a mammoth defensive
tackle want to run and hide. As a coach, he could walk up to a player one
day and hug him and kiss him on the head, yet the very next day give
the same player a blistering dressing-down in front of the entire team.
According to Brad Benson, one of his Giants players, the unique thing
about Parcells is that he is self-assured. "He can be a players' coach, yet
when we get back to the locker room and he has to regain control of the
team, he can do that" (Gutman, 2000, p. 3).

Parcells apparently feels that the dichotomy is necessary, that you
can't have one without the other. "Coaching is about interaction, and
trying to know your players. If you respect a player and he respects you,
then you have a relationship, and in a relationship all commentary is
allowed" (Gutman, 2000, p. 4). According to Dave Jennings, his Giants
punter, even in his first year with the Giants, he reacted to each player
differently. He knew which players he could treat harshly and which
ones were more sensitive and had to be treated accordingly. However,
Jennings believes he always liked the guys who could take a "needling"
better.

Writer Will McDonough recognized Parcells's awareness of the situational nature of leadership when he observed that although Parcells
was strictly a power-football advocate when he coached the Giants,
when he became head coach of the New England Patriots, he switched
to a finesse style of play. When he coached the Giants, he designed the
team specifically so that he could beat the Washington Redskins, who
were bigger and stronger at the line of scrimmage in his first few years.
When he got to New England, he didn't have those kind of players, so
he turned his excellent passing quarterback, Drew Bledsoe, loose and
played the finesse game.

In expressing his positive view of the need for situational leadership,
Parcells recalls that a wise person once observed that inflexibility is
one of the worst human failings. One can learn to check impetuosity,
to overcome fear with confidence and laziness with discipline. But for
rigidity of mind and action, there is no antidote. Inflexibility carries the

seeds of its own destruction. According to Parcells, to succeed over the long haul, leaders must stay true to their own vision and core philosophy. But to flourish in a given situation, "they must also be flexible in strategy and opportunistic in tactics" (Parcells & Coplon, 1995, p. 27).

THE STRUCTURAL FRAME

Structural leaders seek to develop a new model of the relationship between structure, strategy, and environment in their organizations. Strategic planning, extensive preparation, and effecting change are priorities for them. Bill Parcells has a reputation among the public as a strong leader. Translated into theoretical terms, a "strong leader" refers to a leader who primarily utilizes structural frame behavior. As we will see, such a definition aptly describes Bill Parcells.

Like many structural frame types, Parcells has a very intimidating presence with both his players and the public. At press conferences, for example, he can cause the most experienced reporter to feel like a kid failing a journalism course by reacting to the most innocent inquiry with a look of extreme disgust, quickly adding, "Now that was a dumb-ass question" (Gutman, 2000, p. 1). Through it all, though, Bill Parcells has remained steadfast in his never-changing goal: to produce winning football teams good enough to contend for the Super Bowl title. One of his former players, Giants halfback Joe Morris, says, "He is like a general. He has to be in control" (Gutman, 2000, p. 3).

Parcells openly admits that a sensitive athlete has a hard time playing for him. He contends that the only players he hurts with his harsh words are those with an inflated opinion of their ability. "And, I can't worry about that" (Gutman, 2000, p. 3). He is very exacting and, like many structural leaders, requires perfection. One of his former players commented that he was virtually impossible to please. He was never satisfied. The player opined that if Parcells were named king on Sunday, he would be unhappy by Tuesday.

There was no denying, however, that Parcells was a dedicated student of the game. One of his college teammates noted that, even early on, he had a maturity about him, a drive, an instinct, a knowledge and sense of football that others did not possess. He described it as an awareness and knowledge that was several steps above his peers. For example, many coaches run standard drills in practice all the time. They run them because their coaches ran them. However, Parcells emulated his friend Bobby Knight and ran drills with a purpose. He never ran them just for the sake of it.

Parcells indicates that he tried being a less structural coach, but it did not work. When he first became head coach of the Giants in 1983, he tried a kinder, gentler approach and ended the season 3–12–1. So, beginning in 1984, Parcells was going to do it his way. He never wanted to go 3–12–1 again. He would now become the Parcells people would get to know—but not always like. Dave Jennings, his Giants kicker said, "Bill was a different coach right from the start of 1984" (Gutman, 2000, p. 87). By that he meant that Parcells had put his foot down and was much tougher. One could tell the difference right from training camp, and as a result, his players reacted differently to him. Of course, from that season on, the Giants were very successful, and Parcells attached a cause-and-effect relationship to that success and his increased use of structural frame leadership behavior.

True to structural leadership frame advocates, Parcells took charge of situations even when he may not have been truly knowledgeable on the subject. For example, according to Paul McConkey, one of his star kick returners, Parcells would stand next to him in practice and critique him as he was fielding a punt or a kickoff. Parcells never caught a punt in his life, but that did not keep him from critiquing every one of Mc-Conkey's catches and never being quite satisfied. Commenting further on Parcells's demanding ways, McConkey recalls how we might see a football game today when a player slips on the wet Astroturf, goes to the sidelines, and says, "I slipped coach." And the coach accepts it. Parcells might say, "Get some shoes that work" (Gutman, 2000, p. 90).

Parcells used structural frame leadership behavior in dealing with superstar linebacker Laurence Taylor. When drafted by the Giants, Taylor was a great linebacker against the run but knew little about pass defense and the various types of coverages. According to Parcells, at North Carolina, Taylor was so good he was used to intimidating people. Parcells made it clear from the start that intimidating Parcells was just out of the question, and they got along just fine. Taylor was always willing to listen when Parcells spoke and ultimately learned to be a complete player.

Nevertheless, even with these idiosyncrasies, make no mistake about it: Parcells had a well-thought-out plan for success. According to him, when organizations refer to "systems" or "philosophies," they are talking about the same thing. Scratch the surface of any thriving organization, and you will find a defined philosophy. These success stories have integrity and adhere strictly to their organizational principles. Parcells points out that some people fail to realize that it makes no difference what that philosophy is, as long as it meets the following standards:

- It has a sound basis.
- It reflects the leader's vision and values.
- It is communicated and accepted throughout the organization.
- Most importantly, it remains in place long enough to allow success (Parcells, 1995, p. 10).

Parcells points to Wal Mart, General Electric, Bill Walsh, Don Shula, Tom Landry, Jimmy Johnson, Joe Gibbs, and Buddy Ryan. All had different philosophies, which were all successful because they met the above four standards.

So, what is Bill Parcells's philosophy? According to him, it begins with the principle drummed into him during his playing days in high school: aggressive, relentless defense is the key to any sport. You can't be any good if you can't stop the other team. He also believes that good coaching can cut down on penalties and turnovers and that smarter, error-free teams have a better chance of winning, even against more skilled opponents. That's why he is so committed to constant drilling, preparation, and conditioning. In addition, his players don't argue with officials, taunt opponents, or celebrate their own play on the field. He wants a team that is in good physical condition, that plays to its strengths, is mentally tough, and responds at the point of the game when winning or losing is determined.

However, Parcells is not such a perfectionist that he does not make room for error. He accepts false steps as opportunities to learn. It's one thing to hate failure; it's quite another to fear it. He points to his own experience to make his point. If he had feared failure, he would never have taken the foundering New England Patriots job. When one tries a play that backfires, it's always an education: either the concept was

flawed, or the execution needs work, or both. He concludes, "If you succeed every time, you're not risking" (Gutman, 2000, p. 76).

Like most structural leaders, Parcells demands accountability. But
he believes that accountability starts at the top. One cannot build an
accountable organization without leaders who take full responsibility.
Leaders have to work harder than the people they hope to motivate.
Suffice it to say, Bill Parcells is a leader in the structural mode.

THE HUMAN RESOURCE FRAME

Human resource leaders believe in people and communicate that belief.
They are passionate about *productivity through people*. Although Bill
Parcells is far from the warm-and-cuddly personality type often associated with human resource frame leaders, there is evidence that he utilizes this frame of leadership behavior more frequently than one would
think. He must have had at least a somewhat close personal relationship
with his players in light of the fact that his New York Giants Super Bowl
winners had the courage to douse him with Gatorade after the final
whistle, which was the beginning of the tradition that is so familiar to
sports fans today.

A number of his former players, like Willie McGinest of the Patriots,
claimed that along with the yelling and discipline, Parcells had a softer
side and that he and other players became very close to their coach.
McGinest said, "Me and Bill were tight and that's not just as a coach.
He was also a friend" (Gutman, 2000, p. 6). Similarly, George Martin,
who was on his New York Giants team, depicted Parcells as one who
was great at "fireside chatter." Parcells would pull his players aside and
have private conversations with them. He used these "conversations" to
give the players a behind-the-scenes look at what he was trying to do
strategically. According to Martin, Parcells did this daily, especially with
those whom he considered leaders. Still another of his former players,
Dave Jennings, remembered that he and Parcells had become friends
and really got to know each other by playing racquetball together during
the off-season.

Parcells admittedly sees the need to complement structural leadership behavior with human resource behavior. He says, "Coaching is

about human interactions and trying to know your players. If you respect a player and he respects you, then you have a fruitful relationship" (Gutman, 2000, p. 71). Harry Carson, one of his star players, observed that Parcells was forever trying to find ways of getting to each player. That often meant doing some homework. It meant talking to the player's friends and former coaches. For instance, he found out what Carson's nickname had been as a kid. One day he came up to him and whispered the nickname in his ear. It was a nickname that Carson didn't want him yelling out to the whole team, but it got his attention. "But the funny thing was that it told me that the guy cared enough to dig into who I was" (Gutman, 2000, p. 87). Parcells was particularly careful to praise those who play a supporting role and are often overlooked.

Despite taking verbal abuse from his coach on a regular basis, Phil Simms believes that Parcells was very down-to-earth and communicated with his players very well. Simms believes that this human touch separated him from a lot of other coaches in the NFL. Brad Benson of the Giants provides another example. Benson had jumped offsides on a key play. After the game, the team got on a plane for the trip back to New York. He and Parcells didn't talk initially, but later in the flight, the coach sent for Benson. Benson was thinking the worst, but when he arrived at Parcells's seat, the coach simply said, "Well, you know I love you. Just forget the whole thing. Now go back and sit down" (Gutman, 2000, p. 107).

Ever the practical man, Parcells utilized human resource leadership behavior because, in his estimation, it paid dividends. He had a philosophy of never asking people to do things that were beyond them. For example, his 1993 Patriots team, like his 1983 Giants, were just not ready to perform at a consistently high level. His job was to keep the game close, then try to win it at the end. He believed that if he had repeatedly asked these teams to execute plays beyond their ability, he would have cost them some games and hurt their confidence to take more manageable risks in the future. So, he decided to utilize human resource rather than structural leadership behavior with these teams. He acted as a teacher instead of a drill sergeant. In the process, he might overcoach a player, might discuss things a little longer than was necessary, but the player would know that Parcells appreciated his limitations and would help him overcome them.

According to Harry Carson, Parcells always liked to get on Jim Burt, another linebacker. Burt was a solid player but also a practical joker, and the two would often pull pranks on one another. It was Carson and Burt who grabbed the bucket of Gatorade after a Super Bowl win, walked up behind Parcells, and when he took his headphone off, drenched him. It was the first time this was done to any coach. By 1986, it had taken on a life of its own. Suffice it to say, Parcells had a very human side to his overall autocratic persona.

THE SYMBOLIC FRAME

In the symbolic frame, the organization is seen as a stage, a theater in which every actor plays certain roles, and the symbolic leader attempts to communicate the right impressions to the right audiences. Like most of his coaching counterparts, Bill Parcells utilized the symbolic frame of leadership quite astutely. His symbolic behavior was all about building a tough guy image. According to Phil McConkey, the team could be having the greatest practice session, but if that happened to be the day Parcells wanted to call it off early, tell them that they were no darn good, and send them in, he would do it, no matter how good the practice was. He had simply decided that it was "Message Day" (Gutman, 2000, p. 96). George Martin, another of his great linebackers, believes that Parcells's hardnose image was something he created by design. According to Martin, he felt he could use it to his advantage. He didn't want people to see that "beneath that gruff exterior lies a human being" (Gutman, 2000, p. 130). Along these same lines, halfback Keith Byars said that Parcells was partial to wide receivers who didn't wear gloves or mittens on cold days. The running backs were the old "down-and-dirty workhorses" who could have played in any era. These were "Parcells's guys" (Gutman, 2000, p. 227).

Like many coaches, Parcells was not averse to using symbolic behavior in the locker room to motivate his players. At halftime of a Super Bowl game, he pointed out to his players that if they won a championship, it would be with them for the rest of their lives. "A prime example is the guy last night," he said. "There's still time to win this game" (Gutman,

2000, p. 198). The "guy last night" was Evander Holyfield, who had just knocked out Mike Tyson in one of boxing's monumental upsets.

Another significant example of symbolic behavior in Parcells life is in the origin of his nickname, "the Big Tuna." Parcells picked up the nickname when a player tried to pull something over on him, and he replied, "Who do you think I am, Charlie Tuna?" (Gutman, 2000, p. 200). At the time, Charlie Tuna was a popular cartoonlike character on a certain brand of tuna fish. The press picked it up, and the rest is history.

THE POLITICAL FRAME

Leaders operating out of the political frame clarify what they want and what they can get. Political leaders are realists above all. They never let what they want cloud their judgment about what is possible. They assess the distribution of power and interests. Parcells is a master of political intrigue. He retired from coaching three times, only to be "enticed" into coming back each time. There is one prototypical instance of his use of political frame leadership behavior when he left the New England Patriots after disagreements with owner Robert Kraft. Parcells felt he did not have enough input in player personnel decisions. Upon his departure, Parcells stated, "If they want you to cook the dinner, at least they ought to let you shop for some of the groceries" (Gutman, 2000, p. 189). He was referring mainly to an incident in the Patriots' war room during the 1996 draft. Parcells, who wanted to draft a defensive player with their first-round choice, was vetoed by Kraft, and the Patriots selected a wide receiver.

Although Parcells had decided to leave New England, his contract did not allow him to coach anywhere else. The New York Jets sought Parcells to take over their football operation after a 4–28 record under Rich Kotite. In a blatant use of political frame leadership behavior to circumvent Parcells's contractual obligations, the Jets hired Bill Belichick, Parcells's assistant at New England, as the Jets coach, then hired Bill Parcells in an "advisory" capacity. New England threatened legal action against Parcells and the Jets, but NFL Commissioner Paul Tagliabue brokered a deal between the two sides, with New England releasing Parcells from his contract and the Jets giving New England a first-round draft choice.

CONCLUSION

Although Bill Parcells can best be described as a no-nonsense structural frame leader, there are indications that he has utilized the other three leadership frames. The mere fact that his players felt comfortable enough to pour Gatorade over him for the first time in NFL football history indicates that he must have exhibited some human resource frame leadership behavior in his day-to-day interactions with the team. His allowing himself to be referred to as the Big Tuna and his arrogant treatment of the press are instances of his reliance on symbolic leadership behavior on occasion. Finally, the way he parlayed his success into becoming one of the highest paid and most powerful coaches in the NFL evinces his apt use of political frame leadership behavior. With some prudent tweaking, leaders and aspiring leaders could do far worse than to model their leadership behavior after that of Bill Parcells.

9

ARA PARSEGHIAN

Adversity has the effect of eliciting talent that under more prosperous circumstances would have lain dormant.

—Ara Parseghian

BACKGROUND

Ara Parseghian is known primarily for having coached football at Notre Dame University for eleven years. His time with Notre Dame is popularly known as the Era of Ara. During his seasons as head coach of the Fighting Irish he compiled a 95–17–4 record, making him the most successful Notre Dame coach of the modern era. Previous to his tenure at Notre Dame, he coached football at Miami of Ohio and Northwestern University.

After high school graduation and a stint in the U.S. Navy during World War II, Parseghian played halfback at Miami of Ohio University and had a short pro career with the Cleveland Browns before an injury put an end to his playing days.

His collegiate coaching career began as a graduate assistant under the legendary Woody Hayes at Miami University in 1950. He was elevated to head coach the following year when Hayes left to assume the head coaching job at Ohio State. Parseghian stayed at his alma mater for five years until he was hired by Northwestern University as head football coach. He coached Northwestern from 1956 to 1963, during which time his teams defeated Notre Dame four straight times. His success against Notre Dame did not go unnoticed by the Fighting Irish officials.

In 1963, after a mediocre 5–4 season, Parseghian had a personality clash with the Northwestern athletic director, prompting Parseghian to contact Rev. Edmund Joyce, the famous vice president and athletic director at Notre Dame. Parseghian first made certain that Hugh Devore was still only the interim head coach, and when Joyce affirmed that he was, Parseghian formally applied. Despite being a non-Catholic and not being a Notre Dame alum, like virtually all of his predecessors, he got the job. Parseghian was Notre Dame's twenty-second head coach, inheriting a team that had finished 2–7 in 1963 and taking it to within 1:33 of an undefeated season and a national championship in 1964, his first season at the Fighting Irish helm.

Parseghian was known to have excellent organizational skills, and his ability to put the right players in the right positions led to his success. He developed underutilized talent in quarterback John Huarte and end Jack Snow. They both set numerous school passing and receiving records. Snow and Huarte went on to be All-Americans, and Huarte won the 1964 Heisman Trophy. In a symbolic effort to overcome the losing attitude of the immediate past, Parseghian also eliminated all ornamentation on the player's uniforms, including the players' names. He wanted to emphasize the importance of the team over the individual.

During the "Era of Ara," the Irish won two national championships in 1966 and 1973. In 1969, the Notre Dame administration changed its policy forbidding the team from playing in bowl games. Parseghian led the team to its first bowl game in the modern era, the Cotton Bowl, on January 1, 1970, losing 21–17 to the eventual national champions, the Texas Longhorns. However, despite all of his success at Notre Dame, Parseghian could not quite achieve his dream of an undefeated, untied season. In 1966, he went for a tie rather than a win against Michigan State in one of the most memorable games in college football history. He defended his decision by maintaining that several key starters had been injured early in the game, and he didn't want to spoil a courageous comeback from a 10–0 deficit by risking a turnover deep in his own terri-tory late in the game. Nevertheless, his decision was vindicated when the Fighting Irish were awarded the National Championship that year.

In 1973, Parseghian finally achieved the elusive perfect season, with a thrilling 24–23 victory over Alabama in the Sugar Bowl. He considered retiring on top after that game but decided to stay at Notre Dame for at least one more year. The Irish would have most of their starters back in 1974 and were favored to repeat as national champions. But a number of suspensions and injuries combined to derail Notre Dame's effort to win another National Championship. Parseghian decided to retire at the end of the season for health reasons. Notre Dame's 13–11 win over Alabama in a rematch in the Orange Bowl enabled Parseghian to retire on a winning note.

After retiring from coaching, Parseghian entered private business. He also served as a color analyst for ABC Sports from 1975 to 1981 and for CBS Sports from 1982 to 1988. He was inducted into the College Football Hall of Fame in 1980 (La Monte & Shook, 2004; Pagna & Par-seghian, 1976; Wikipedia.org).

SITUATIONAL LEADERSHIP ANALYSIS

Situational models of leadership differ from earlier trait and behavioral models in asserting that no single way of leading works in all situations. Rather, appropriate behavior depends on the circumstances at a given time. Effective managers diagnose the situation, identify the leader-ship style or behavior that will be most effective, and then determine whether they can implement the required style.

Like most effective leaders, Ara Parseghian realized very early in his career that he had to adjust his leadership behavior to the ever-chang-ing situation in order to be successful. He coached during the turbulent 1960s, when moral and ethical, not to mention dress and grooming, stan-dards were being questioned. The 1960s made Parseghian significantly more tolerant than he had formerly been. He developed a saying: "Give me a reason I can hang my hat on, and I'll accept any logical suggestion" (Pagna & Parseghian, 1976, p. 21). For example, just because a player's hair sticks out of his helmet and the fans joke that he looks like a girl, that's no reason to make him cut his hair, asserted Parseghian. The fact was that he did not like it himself, but he could not defend the logic of those who wanted a player's hair short simply because it looked feminine when it was long. So, he eventually allowed long hair. On the other hand, facial hair could be a hindrance if a player got cut and needed stitches. Parseghian could hang his hat on that, and mustaches were out.

For the first time in his career, Parseghian had players challenging his demeanor. Players would complain that they resented being "screamed at." They didn't think that was right. "I'm a person, and I have feelings," they would say. Although he did not change his basic philosophy of doing whatever the situation called for, Parseghian adjusted to the times. For example, some of his players wanted to participate in a "Stop the War" demonstration. He responded that if they felt in the depths of their hearts that doing so was meaningful to them, he would have no objection. He did caution them, however, to make sure it was a peaceful demonstration and admonished them, "Don't allow yourself to be coerced into doing this" (Pagna & Parseghian, 1976, p. 161).

Parseghian adjusted his leadership behavior to the situation in the way he used his personnel. He was known as a very conservative coach, which he was when he had talented players on whom he could depend to execute the fundamentals more effectively than the opposition. However, in the seasons when he did not have a plethora of talent, he tried everything. In those years, he would show hundreds of different formations to confuse the opposition. He would use quick huddles, slow cadences, draw plays, screens, reverses, and double reverses. His guiding principle was always, "Take the personnel, see what they can do best, and let them dictate strategy. Don't start with the strategy first" (Pagna & Parseghian, 1976, p. 36). After a few years of experience, he was able to come up with a style of play that suited any personnel.

From these few examples, we can readily see that Ara Parseghian was quite adept at adjusting his leadership behavior to the situation.

THE STRUCTURAL FRAME

Structural leaders seek to develop a new model of the relationship between structure, strategy, and environment in their organizations. Strategic planning, extensive preparation, and effecting change are priorities for them. Ara Parseghian was well-known as a rather strict disciplinarian. He believed that during the 1960s, Notre Dame football was one of the last bastions of discipline left in the United States. According to him, the military no longer had the strict discipline that it once had; nor did schools, churches, or families. He believed that athletics might be the only area left where a young man or women, for two hours or so a day, yielded him- or herself to a coach out of a desperate desire to be part of a team. We tell a football player "to discipline himself so that he loses himself for something bigger—the team" (Pagna & Parseghian, 1976, p. 21).

Parseghian believed that an organized coach could overcome any obstacle. For example, in the early 1960s, he became very conservative in his approach to football. Instead of creating a large repertoire of plays, he decided to concentrate on a few basic patterns and execute them to perfection. The opposition might have an idea of what his team would do, but if his team did it well enough, it would be up to the opposition to try to stop them. His preparation and organization were such that not many of them could.

As with so many structural leaders, Parseghian was demanding of both his players and his staff. He wanted his assistant coaches in at 7 a.m. each morning for their staff meetings. They worked until noon, then broke for lunch. At 1 p.m., they were back together and stayed that way until practice at 3 p.m. After the workouts, they always ate with the team, then met with them by positions, but they weren't finished yet. It was back to Parseghian's office until 10 p.m., when they finally got to go home "and remind our families who we were" (Pagna & Parseghian, 1976, p. 63).

In a prototypical structural leader way, Parseghian often reminded his team and staff not to look ahead. To him, there was no game more important than the one being played that day. "What's the good of thinking about next week's game if we lose today?" he would say (Pagna & Parseghian, 1976, p. 71). To his assistants, he would preach that sitting around won't lead to success. We've got to keep striving. We've got to recruit good players, explore new ideas, improve old techniques, and know, really know, the players, he would reiterate.

In another display of structural behavior, Parseghian advised his players that they would not play a day for Notre Dame, not one play, if they did not remain academically eligible. He told them to let him know if they were having trouble in class, and he would find a tutor. "But, by God, I won't go to bat for you if you're not in class" (Pagna & Parseghian, 1976, p. 53).

Lack of effort was another of his pet peeves. He had no use for a player who gave less than 100 percent. And when one analyzed his requirements, there really was no reason for a player to "dog it." Parseghian had a concept that he called "Great Interval." The interval was effort, execution, and endurance. His premise was that each play of a football game lasts an average of 3.5 seconds, and there are approximately eighty offensive and defensive plays in a game. This works out to about five minutes of action. So, he put it to the players, "Can you give Our Lady of Notre Dame five minutes of your effort, execution, and endurance today" (Pagna & Parseghian, 1976, p. 198)? Leave it to a structural leader to go through the trouble to figure something like that out.

THE HUMAN RESOURCE FRAME

Human resource leaders believe in people and communicate that belief. They are passionate about *productivity through people.* A number of instances demonstrate Ara Parseghian's affinity for using human resource frame leadership behavior, not only with his own team but with the opposition. After a national championship victory over Southern California, he advised his players that when the press walked into the locker room, he did not want to hear his players in any way criticize their opponent. "I don't want you to alibi. I don't want you to show any emotion or temperament other than those of young gentlemen" (Pagna & Parseghian, 1976, p. 20). He was careful to follow the same rules himself.

One of his players at Miami of Ohio, Tom Pagna, voiced his sentiments about the effect of Parseghian's use of human resource behavior. "It's funny, I loved Miami of Ohio, and I always will. But whenever I suited up, I was playing for Ara Parseghian, not Miami." According to Pagna, this loyalty was also true for his teammates. "Ara seemed to affect people that way" (Pagna & Parseghian, 1976, p. 31). Later, when Parseghian was considering Pagna for an assistant coaching position at Miami of Ohio, Parseghian cautioned him that despite wanting desperately to hire him, his own position there was a little "shaky." He had only one more year left on his contract, and his record had not been very good. He would have hated to see Pagna move his family only to wind up without a job in a year. Of course, knowing Parseghian's sense of integrity, Pagna took the job anyway.

Another of Parseghian's assistant coaches relates the time when he became bothered by the lack of compliments from Parseghian. Parseghian responded to his grievance by pointing out that looking at it from that perspective was building an "employee-employer relationship," and that was not what he was all about. Parseghian preferred a family relationship, where they were all in it together. It just so happened that fate dictated that he "called the shots." But the staff was as much a part of the program as he was, and any success they had, they would have together. After thinking about it further, the assistant coach saw Parseghian's point and agreed that "by hiring us he paid us the highest compliment of all. He implied confidence in our ability" (Pagna & Parseghian, 1976, p. 147).

Parseghian always had a keen sense of humor, which is typical of a human resource leader. At Miami of Ohio, he had a shot putter on the team named Tom Jones. He could put the shot around fifty-six feet. In 1952, the world record was only sixty feet. During spring practice, Parseghian wanted to have some fun with him, so he had one of the assistant coaches make up a wooden shot and paint it black. They approached Jones hard at work on his specialty. "Gosh, that looks easy," Parseghian began. "I bet any guy with some muscle and half a brain could throw that farther than you." Naturally, Jones challenged Parseghian to a match. Jones's first put was over fifty feet. When the assistant coach went out to measure, he surreptitiously switched shots and brought the wooden one back to Parseghian. Parseghian said that he had never tried shot putting before so he begged Jones for a couple of practice throws. Jones complied, and Parseghian threw two shots of forty-five and fifty-five feet and said, "I think I've got it." Indicating that the next one would count, he proceeded to launch the put over sixty-five feet. Jones finally caught on to the hoax and broke up with the rest of the team.

So, beyond being a taskmaster and psychologist, Parseghian befriended his players. He allowed them to laugh when the laugh was there. He clowned and they clowned when the moment was right. For example, like many colleges, Notre Dame had a tradition that after spring practice ended, the freshman players had to put on a skit for the rest of the team. After a while these rookies understood the tradition and came to the last practice prepared. As it turned out, most of them did impersonations of Parseghian. They'd walk like him, whistle like him, spit like him, yell like him, and maybe even swear like him.

Parseghian's concern for human dignity meant that he would never criticize any of his players in public. Of course, he expected the same in return. He sought to be fair to all of his players and with each member of his staff. In doing so, he hoped that he would gain their respect as a person who genuinely cared about them. He refused to be "placed upon a pedestal" and invited them to address him by his first name if they felt comfortable doing so. None of them ever did however.

Parseghian used the human touch especially when it came to those on the team who did not get recognition from the fans and the media. The game-preparation players rarely suited up for a game and almost never appeared in one. But they showed up faithfully to practice every day like the varsity players and went through the same conditioning with few of the rewards. Parseghian did his best to repay them when he could, dressing as many as possible and taking some on the road when there were openings.

As mentioned earlier, Parseghian always took a deep interest in the educational progress of his players. He knew as well as anyone that playing football is a temporary activity. His involvement in their academic progress wasn't just peripheral. He worked closely with the academic counselors to see to it that his players were getting to class and making the required effort. He really cared that they have a life after football.

One of his more famous players at Notre Dame, Rocky Bleir, was severely wounded in Vietnam. After his discharge from the U.S. Army, he returned to Notre Dame for the 1969 Southern California game to be honored during the halftime ceremonies. He limped badly and needed a cane for support. Even though Fridays before home games were hectic, Parseghian made sure that he found plenty of time to spend with Rocky.

Another of his players at Notre Dame, Jim Lynch, team captain in 1966 and then a member of the Kansas City Chiefs, attested to Parseghian's use of human resource behavior. He opined that to be part of Notre Dame is to be part of a tradition much bigger that any one man, one team, or one season. According to Lynch, Parseghian embodied the quality that will always describe Notre Dame: class. Under him, players learned how to win and how to lose. Simply put, "Ara is the finest man I have ever been associated with" (Pagna & Parseghian, 1976, p. 258).

THE SYMBOLIC FRAME

In the symbolic frame, the organization is seen as a stage, a theater in which every actor plays certain roles, and the symbolic leader attempts to communicate the right impression to the right audiences. Coaching at Notre Dame can be described as the definition of symbolism. That Notre Dame mystique is well established, and Ara Parseghian exploited it masterfully to his program's advantage.

Parseghian was prolific in his use of slogans, quotes, and epigraphs to motivate his team. His favorites included

> Fame is a vapor
> Popularity an accident
> Riches take wings
> Those that cheer you today
> Will curse you tomorrow
> One thing endures . . . character.
> —Horace Greeley

and

> Adversity has the effect of eliciting talent that under more prosperous circumstances would have lain dormant. (Pagna & Parseghian, 1976, p. 18)

Another was

> To be great, to achieve, you must pay the price. You must earn the right. This is true of everything in life. Everything worthwhile must be bought with sacrifice.

Finally, the following words were on a sign at the locker room exit:

> What Tho the Odds
> Be They Great or Small
> Notre Dame Men
> Win, Win Over All!

Those were the last written words the players saw before they took the field, and they would tap the sign with their hands as they passed under it.

Another instance of Parseghian's use of symbolic leadership behavior took place against Alabama in the Orange Bowl before the last game he coached. "Win this game," he said. "Let's show them why we're Notre Dame and the tradition we have. This will be the last time I walk out of this locker room with you and I want this win. I want it for Notre Dame. Let's get out there!" (Pagna & Parseghian, 1976, p. 13).

Despite not being Roman Catholic, Parseghian used religiously oriented symbolic behavior to motivate his team. "I know we're not of the same religious persuasion," he told his players, "but I think the Lord's Prayer ought to cover everyone. As we prayed and were reaching out to each other, we felt tremendous unity. It really had an effect as we ran out onto the field" (Pagna & Parseghian, 1976, p. 31). From then on, his teams said the Lord's Prayer before every game.

Attending Mass before each game was a longstanding Notre Dame tradition before Parseghian arrived. He insisted on retaining the tradition, and he, too, went to the Masses. He continued to do so until the late 1960s, then missed two weeks in a row. When he found out that twenty or thirty of the players also stayed away, he got angry. After analyzing it, however, he realized it wasn't right to insist that they go if he was absent. He never missed a service thereafter.

One of Parseghian's assistant coaches remembered his first year at Notre Dame. Before the season, pep rallies at which the students carried lighted torches were held on a daily basis leading up to the first game. The torch rallies continued for weeks. The students implored Parseghian nightly to come out of the Rockne Building and address them. Finally, he did, and that was all it took to win them forever. The students listened and loved him. "If he talks to you, you're his," said one of the students (Pagna & Parseghian, 1976, p. 47).

Parseghian reinforced the value of teamwork by using symbols. He had drilled into his team that it takes teamwork to win. Then, he showed them his fist. When someone makes a fist, it's strong and difficult to tear it apart. As long as there is unity, he constantly reminded them, there is strength. So, how do we accomplish success, he would ask? You've got to make a believer out of me that you want to be football players! And I've got to make you believe I am the best capable leader for you!

When he first arrived at Notre Dame, they had experienced successive years of failure. Parseghian reminded them immediately of the great football tradition at Notre Dame. That tradition, he pointed out, was why most of them came to Notre Dame. Notre Dame teams "had a fire that blazed the sky in the past" (Pagna & Parseghian, 1976, p. 48). Perhaps the flame has burned low as of late, but it is nowhere near out.

Another instance of Parseghian's use of symbolic leadership behavior came in an excruciating last-second defeat at the hands of their archrival, Southern California, to lose a perfect season and the national championship. "Dear God, give us the strength in our moment of despair to understand and accept that which we have undergone," he said to the team (Pagna & Parseghian, 1976, p. 75). Then he went on to tell them that he wanted them to realize one thing. What they did there and then would follow them for many years. There were thousands of things they could say. They could blame the officials and their calls. But when they won that year, they had won as Notre Dame men—fair, hard, and with humility. To be less than that at this moment, to cry foul, to alibi, would undo much of what that season had been. For the next ten minutes, he told them, no one would be allowed in the locker room. If you've got to scream, if you want to cry, swear, or punch the locker, do it now, he said. He could understand all those sentiments. But after the doors were opened, he wanted all of them to hold their tongues, lift their heads high, and in the face of defeat be Notre Dame men. He reminded them that he had never been associated with a greater bunch of athletes. "No one will ever forget the achievement you made this year" (Pagna & Parseghian, 1976, p. 75).

Another instance of Parseghian's use of symbolic leadership behavior involved Mike McGill and Jim Seymour, two of his Notre Dame stars, being injured in the first half of the Oklahoma game. At halftime in the locker room, the players were yelling, "They've hurt us. Those guys have hurt use. Let's go out and get even!" Parseghian said, "No one hates seeing a player hurt more than I. It is the stinking part of the game no one can control. But whatever you feel, play clean." According to him, the worst thing that you could do to any team was beat them. "Let's do it hard and clean," he said (Pagna & Parseghian, 1976, p. 109).

Parseghian utilized symbolic behavior in his recruitment policies also. His underlying doctrine was that there was never a need to violate the rules in any recruitment activity. He believed that nothing could be gained from doing so. He did not want the kind of kid who had to be bought to play for him.

Parseghian also knew that the outcome of symbolic behavior had to be placed in perspective. He remembered the adversity that the Notre Dame fans experienced before he came there in 1964. But after he had won his first five or six games, the students became drunk with their newfound power. During one game late in the season, it began to snow, and the students started chanting, "Ara, stop the snow! Ara, stop the snow!" Parseghian walked over to one of his assistants with a puzzled expression and said, "That's ridiculous!" He paused for a moment, gazed back quizzically, and asked, "Do you think I *could*?"

However, just to show how the years change a person, during a game ten years later, it was snowing off and on, and at one point, the students renewed the cry of their predecessors: "Ara, stop the snow!" This time, there was no hesitancy in his voice as he asked his assistant, "Do you think I *should*?" (Pagna & Parseghian, 1976, p. 156).

It should be obvious from these many examples that Ara Parseghian was a master at using symbolic leadership behavior.

THE POLITICAL FRAME

Leaders operating out of the political frame clarify what they want and what they can get. Political leaders are realists above all. They never let what they want cloud their judgment about what is possible. They assess the distribution of power and interests.

Albeit infrequently, Ara Parseghian utilized the political frame when appropriate. For example, he addressed his daughter Karan's multiple sclerosis diagnosis in typical Parseghian fashion. Like any other obstacle in his life, as soon as he found out what it was, he made up his mind to go out and conquer it. He learned all he could about multiple sclerosis. Money was the bottom line for research. So, he threw himself into a money-raising campaign whereby he used every contact that he had made during his career to help defeat this new foe. That commitment continues today.

Parseghian used political frame leadership behavior in another, foot-ball-related instance. He had championed the cause of participating in bowl games since he came to Notre Dame. Through sheer perseverance and by demonstrating the opportunity to claim a national championship, not to mention the money that these games would generate for the university, he convinced Notre Dame's administration to let the school's teams participate in postseason bowl games.

Finally, Parseghian also used political leadership behavior more subtly. He was convinced that officials could be swayed, just by virtue of human nature. He always made some comment to them when a close call went the other way. He realized nothing could be done about that particular decision, but arguing might give them second thoughts, inducing them to see a future call his way.

CONCLUSION

Ara Parseghian is an outstanding example of a leader who appropriately utilizes all four of the leadership frames recommended by Lee Bolman and Terrence Deal. He was well organized, thoroughly prepared, and very goal-oriented—all traits of a structural frame leader. He was also sensitive to the needs of his players and staff and applies a human touch in his leadership behavior. His effectiveness in his appropriate application of human resource leadership behavior was borne out by the loyalty that he engendered in his players and assistant coaches, which endured years after their careers were over.

We saw many instances where he appropriately utilized symbolic leadership behavior and inspired his players to perform oftentimes beyond their capabilities. He also used symbolic frame leadership behavior to send "messages" to his team about how he wanted them to behave in various situations. Finally, he used political frame leadership behavior when appropriate. Although he did so sparingly, he used it skillfully when the situation demanded it. In summary, Ara Parseghian is someone whom we can emulate if we wish to be effective leaders.

10

JOE PATERNO

The purpose of college football is to serve education, not the other way around.

—Joe Paterno

BACKGROUND

Born in 1926 in Brooklyn, New York, Joe Paterno is the longtime head football coach at Penn State University. He has held the position since 1966. A Hall of Fame coach, Paterno has, along with Bobby Bowden (Chapter 4), won more Division I football games than any other coach in history. He also has more bowl game wins and more undefeated seasons than any other coach in college football history.

In 1944, Paterno graduated from Brooklyn Prep and matriculated at Brown University. There, he was a capable but unspectacular quarterback and cornerback. He gave up an opportunity to attend Law School to go into coaching immediately after graduation in 1950, joining Hall of Famer Rip Engle at Penn State as an assistant coach. In 1966, he succeeded Engle as the head coach at Penn State and ultimately became one of the most famous and recognizable coaches in any sport in the United States.

In 2008, at age eighty-two, Paterno coached his fifty-ninth season at Penn State as an assistant or head coach. The 2008 season marked his forty-third as head coach of the Nittany Lions, passing Amos Alonzo Stagg's record for the most years at a single institution. He recently signed a contract extension virtually ensuring him a job for life at Penn State.

Over the years, Paterno has turned down several coaching positions, including an offer to coach the Pittsburgh Steelers in 1969. In 1972 he also turned down a head coaching position with the New England Patriots, which included a percentage ownership in the team.

As mentioned earlier, Paterno has more bowl victories (twenty-three) than any coach in history. He also tops the list of bowl appearances with thirty-five. He is the only coach to have won each of the current four major bowls—Rose, Orange, Fiesta, and Sugar.

Overall, Paterno has led Penn State to two national championships (1982 and 1986) and five undefeated, untied seasons. Four of his unbeaten teams won major bowl games but were not awarded a national championship.

In 2005, following an 11–1 comeback season in which the Lions won a share of the Big Ten title and a BCS berth, Paterno was named the 2005 Associated Press Coach of the Year. On May 16, 2006, Paterno was elected to the College Football Hall of Fame after the National Football Foundation decided to change its rules and extend eligibility to any coach over the age of seventy-five rather than having to wait until retirement. However, he was injured during a sideline collision. Thus, he was unable to travel to the induction ceremonies in New York City, so the National Football Foundation announced that he would instead be inducted as part of the Hall of Fame Class of 2007.

In addition to his legacy as a coach, Paterno is highly known for his contributions to academics. In 1966, Paterno immediately announced that he would conduct what he called a "Grand Experiment" in melding athletics and academics in the collegiate environment, a concept that developed from his years in the Ivy League. As a result, Penn State's players have consistently achieved a higher degree of academic success than their Division I-A counterparts. In fact, over the past five years, the Nittany Lions' graduation rate has been the highest in the country three times.

Paterno is also renowned for his charitable contributions at Penn State. He and his wife, Sue, have contributed over $4 million to various departments and colleges, including support for the Pasquerilla Spiritual Center, which opened in 2003, and the Penn State All-Sports Museum, which opened in 2002. After helping raise over $13.5 million in funds for the 1997 expansion of Pattee Library, the university named the expansion Paterno Library in their honor (Paterno, 1959, 2007; Paterno & Asbell, 1989; Wikipedia.org).

SITUATIONAL LEADERSHIP ANALYSIS

At age eighty-two, Joe Paterno has been criticized for being too set in his ways and not being situational in his leadership practice. The evidence, however, challenges this observation. For example, one of the perennial objections to the sport of football is that youngsters are susceptible to serious injuries. Today, however, fatalities are very rare and very seldom the direct result of football. Even the number of injuries has declined because the equipment and coaching are better, the rules protect the players, and the coaches do a better job of getting the kids in condition to play. Paterno has been at the forefront of initiating these changes. "In the old days," he says, "we'd never even give a kid water. It's amazing that more kids didn't die of heat exhaustion" (Paterno & Asbell, 1989, p. 61).

He used the situational approach to leadership in regard to his disciplining of two of his players. It seems that he caught two of his players drinking at a hotel bar after a bowl game victory over Miami. One of the players had been in trouble in the past and was summarily dismissed from the team. To the other player, he said, "This is the first trouble I know about. You get one more chance, but you're suspended for the next two games" (Paterno & Asbell, 1989, p. 115).

Paterno became aware of the need to be situational in one's leadership approach early on in his career. Upon assuming the head coaching position at Penn State, he inherited his predecessor's approach to coaching, which had been successful for him. However, after using Rip Engle's coaching philosophies in his first year at the helm, Paterno experienced a losing season. He immediately knew that it would be futile to follow the same philosophy and expect different results. So, he deemed it imperative for him to change. With disaster staring him in the face, he decided that if he wanted to survive in the competitive world of college football, he had to do something radical. He had to do no less than rethink and redesign how a football team ought to play defense. As a result, he created a defensive strategy, novel at the time, called "rotating coverage" whereby he had his defensive backs rotate to the ball, similar to how baseball players back each other up when they field the ball.

Paterno became famous for adapting his game to his personnel, identifying his players' unique talents, and placing them in positions where they could use those individual talents successfully—even when it meant changing their positions. For example, when a great college linebacker showed up at Penn State as a big 198-pound freshman in 1967 after playing offensive guard in high school, Paterno converted him to linebacker because he saw the talent in him for it. After having an All-American career at Penn State, Jack Ham ended up in the Pro Football Hall of Fame as a linebacker. John Cappelletti provides another example of Paterno's ease in practicing situational leadership. Recruited as a linebacker, Cappelletti ended up a Heisman Trophy–winning running back.

However, Paterno sometimes learned the hard way about the appropriate application of situational leadership behavior. In a 1979 game against Alabama University for the national championship, faced with a fourth and goal, his assistant coaches recommended a conservative approach. Paterno's initial reaction was, "That's a lot of crap. This is the time to surprise them and throw the football" (Paterno & Asbell, 1989, p. 215). Unfortunately, Paterno capitulated and ran the ball, and Penn State was stopped on the one-yard line.

But Paterno was a quick learner. Four years later, he faced a similar situation. This time he called for a pass that won the game. "That moment's decision had come easier for me than on New Year's Day, 1979, because I was not the same person I was then" (Paterno & Asbell, 1989 p. 231). He believed that when he had faced Bear Bryant four years before on the very same spot, he wasn't "big enough, strong enough, grown enough" to face the ridicule if they had thrown the ball, it had been intercepted, and they had lost the game. This time, as he said, he was not that same person.

Another instance of Joe Paterno's use of situational leadership behavior occurred after Penn State had three poor seasons immediately following an undefeated season. In addition to a lack of success on the field, team discipline was eroding in that several players got into off-field trouble. This situation told Paterno that he had to reexamine his role as surrogate father to many of his players. He admitted that one reason for the losing seasons and lack of discipline was that he had relaxed his intensity, and the "kids had lost fear and respect of Joe Paterno" (Paterno & Asbell, 1989, p. 216).

Paterno came to understand that in the cycle of leadership styles, there is a time for letting go, for giving people room to move, to make their own mistakes and grow. And there is a time for tightening the reins and getting a team into a single, unified rhythm. Over a span of years, therefore, the more his staff of assistant coaches grew, the more he released his grip and gave them room to develop the players according to their instincts, to analyze the opponents for themselves, and to call their own plays on the field. Paterno had learned the art of situational leadership.

Finally, although he was accused of never adjusting to the changing times, the reality was that he almost always did. The "situationality" of his leadership behavior accounts for the fact that despite having some "down" times, his teams have always come back to their former glory. As recently as two years ago, his team was contending for the national championship following several years of futility when the conventional wisdom held that "the game had passed him by."

THE STRUCTURAL FRAME

Structural leaders seek to develop a new model of the relationship between structure, strategy, and environment in their organizations. Strategic planning, extensive preparation, and effecting change are priorities for them. Joe Paterno has a well-earned reputation for the extensive use of structural frame leadership behavior. He is known as a coach who is always well prepared and demanding of his players, both on the field and in the classroom. One of the reasons for his great success in postseason bowl games is that with the extra two or three weeks that he has to prepare, he almost always outcoaches his opponents.

Paterno learned the value of structural leadership behavior in his formative years. He often alludes to the fact that his father drilled two important attitudes into him: (1) education is really important, and (2) winning isn't as important as having fun. However, while his father's caring for people around him shaped Paterno to some extent, he attributes his drive and intensity to his mother. His mother never took a backseat to anyone, in any place, at any time, according to Paterno. If she couldn't be at the head of the pack, she was not satisfied. "So, as her first son, in anything I did, I had to be at the top. If we had a classroom spelling bee, I was expected to win it" (Paterno & Asbell, 1989, p. 29).

Paterno speculates that he got his sense of rigid discipline from his mother also. He recalls a day at school when he got into a little "chalk-throwing" contest while the nun's back was turned. The nun gave him a smart swat across the knuckles with her ruler. When he got home, his mother wanted to know why his hand was so red. "Sister hit me," was his reply.

"Sister hit you?"

"Yeah, but I didn't do any—"

His mother gave him a shot across the head. "That's for giving Sister problems," she said (Paterno & Asbell, 1989, p. 30).

The value of structural behavior was further drilled into Paterno in high school at Brooklyn Prep. Starting with his first day, his Latin teacher, Father Bermingham, always kept an eye out for kids who had begun what he called the most important task in education: their self-education. Virgil's *Aeneid* was their first project. Paterno complained that translating the four hundred Latin pages was impossible to accomplish in one semester. "What's important," Father Bermingham said, "is not how much we cover. In fact, I don't like that word, 'cover'. It's not how much we do, but the *excellence* of what we do that counts" (Paterno & Asbell, 1989, p. 41).

It was at that point that Virgil's hero, Aeneas, the founder of Rome, entered Paterno's life. Aeneas led his people from Troy to Italy after the Greeks conquered Troy. Paterno decided to model his life after that of Aeneas and his "fate," or "destiny," as a leader. Aeneas, as Virgil created him, is a totally new kind of epic hero. Like Homer's heroes (e.g., Achilles), he endures battles, storms, shipwrecks, and the rages of the gods. But the worst storm is the one that rages within. He yearns to be free of his tormenting duty, but he knows that his duty is to others, to his men. Through years of hardship and peril, Aeneas reluctantly but relentlessly heeds his "fate," or "destiny," until he founds Rome. Paterno saw Aeneas not as a grandstanding superstar but as a Trojan and a Roman. His first commitment is not to himself, but to others. He is bothered constantly by the reminder that his "fate" is to be a man for others. He lives life not for "me" and "I" but for "us" and "we." According to Paterno, "Aeneas is the ultimate team man" (Paterno & Asbell, 1989, p. 46).

This initial tendency toward structural behavior was reinforced later in life. At Brown University, the romantic period of literature held Paterno's interest the most. He considers himself a "romantic," dreaming of gladiators and knights winning battles. He was partial to the movie *Patton*, which depicted Gen. George Patton as a tough-minded lover of poetry and epics, believing that he was reincarnated and in his past life had been a Roman general. "My kind of guy," says Paterno (Paterno & Asbell, 1989, p. 49).

Paterno credits his predecessor at Penn State, Rip Engle, and his high school coach, Gus Zitrides, with teaching him to analyze a problem and put down a specific plan for getting from here to there, step by step, in the time available. The best teacher, according to Paterno, is not the person who has the most knowledge but the one who has the knowledge best organized and can state what he or she knows in coherent ways. If a student doesn't get it when it is taught one way, you've got to teach it another way, he believes. Sometimes great players who become coaches don't get it straight that they are there not because they know how to do it but because they know how to teach it.

According to Paterno, most football fans minimize the importance of structural leadership behavior. No matter how often fans may say, "Yes, I know," Paterno has observed that most of them don't know, and really don't want to know, the importance of attitude, of a clear focus on a goal, of psyching up to attain it, of sustained discipline, of systematically building self-confidence, and of each player's taking responsibility for his own play. Paterno takes a page out of Vince Lombardi's book by pointing out that practice doesn't make perfect; perfect practice makes perfect.

In a typical structural leadership attitude, Paterno welcomes improvements in his opponents as a motive for improving his organization.

"When in some seasons, we're way ahead of the pack, we get careless. Doesn't everybody?" He points out further that "the human tendency, when the competition is better, is to get better" (Paterno & Asbell, 1989, p. 63).

Along these lines of respecting one's opponent, Paterno opines that football is played, above all, with the heart and mind. It's played with the body only secondarily. A coach's first duty is to coach minds. If the coach doesn't succeed in that, the team will not reach its potential. Athletes look to their coaches for examples in struggling to learn poise, class, respect, and the handling of adversity. If confidence and poise are essential to great players, they are at least as important to coaches, according to Paterno. "We cannot convince a football team that they have greatness in them unless they smell self-confidence in us" (Paterno & Asbell, 1989, p. 82). Paterno recalled that when Bear Bryant, among the great coaches of all time, walked out on the football field, self-confidence hung in the air around him like a fine mist.

Paterno is a realist, however, regarding the limits of structural leadership behavior. People often ask him if he concurs with Vince Lombardi's idea that "winning isn't everything, it's the only thing." He responds that he believes in playing as if winning is the only thing, but he never forgets that the opposing coach and the other team are going for the same victory. They cannot control all the tides of fate, and neither can he. So, despite wishing it were otherwise, he knows that many things are not in his control, and he has to learn to live with that. He harks back to the words of his Brooklyn Prep teacher, Father Bermingham, who used to say, "Always work as though everything depended on you. Yet always pray knowing that everything depends on God" (Paterno & Asbell, 1989, p. 120).

In typical structural leader fashion, Paterno often describes sloppiness as a disease. No one ever built a great organization just worrying about the big things. It's the little things that give you the edge, he points out. If the equipment man, for example, in the locker room doesn't check his equipment properly, the player senses it, and the sloppiness gets into his blood stream, and the "disease" spreads. Along these lines, Paterno believes that concentration is the most fragile thing that he knows of. In his view, a team that loses it can't win.

As a result of his structural leadership leanings, Paterno can be a difficult and demanding coach. In a rather humorous vein, Joe Lally, one of his star players, came back to campus after ten years to attend an alumni golf outing. As a memento of the event, all the golf balls had Paterno's face printed on them. Lally said, "I could hardly wait to tee up so I could hit Joe. But you know, it was just like when he was on the practice field. I just looked at the ball—and it started to yell at me" (Paterno & Asbell, 1989, p. 221).

THE HUMAN RESOURCE FRAME

Human resource leaders believe in people and communicate that belief. They are passionate about *productivity through people*. Although he is basically a structural leader, Paterno knows the value of utilizing human resource leadership frame behavior when appropriate. For example, former All-Pro linebacker Jack Ham recalled that "Joe Pa" was always in his face. But, when he was inducted into the Football Hall of Fame in 1988, Ham said, "It only took me about five seconds to decide on Paterno to present me" (Paterno & Asbell, 1989, p. ix).

It was this lack of the human touch that dissuaded Paterno from accepting a professional football coaching job. "I don't like the pros," he said. "They play only to win. There is no other reason to play. Even more than pro players are compelled to win, coaches are compelled to win" (Paterno & Asbell, 1989, p. 12).

Paterno learned the importance of human resource leadership behavior as a very young man. He says that nothing was more important to his parents than family. His father would barely manage the means to send the children to summer camp for a couple of weeks, and his mother would say, "We can't send Joe and George without sending cousin Nicky" (Paterno & Asbell, 1989, p. 28). Nicky's parents could not afford to send him to camp that year, so Paterno's parents found a way to "foot the bill" for him also.

His attitude toward human resource behavior affected his views on racial, religious, and ethnic prejudices also. Athletes were pariahs at Brown University, an academically prestigious Ivy League institution.

"What I felt in those days from some Brownie snobs was exactly what I feel today from some people who clamp shut their white jaws in the presence of a black stranger, silently, eloquently, scarily expressing their superiority" (Paterno & Asbell, 1989, p. 52). His being taken at times for a "football animal" sensitized him to a lifelong empathy with black people.

However, Paterno also recalls failing to apply human resource behavior, which he has since corrected. He remembers when he first became athletic director at Penn State and was very condescending with regard to women's new interest in competitive sports. He said at the time that their participation was a "fad" that would soon dissipate. His attitude was "throw them a crumb," and they will go away. He admits now that he was wrong. Today, women compete at the highest levels and have proven themselves under the full stress of competition.

Paterno attributes much of what he learned about the appropriate application of human resource leadership behavior from his predecessor and mentor at Penn State, Rip Engle. Engle often pointed out to Paterno that people usually don't mind not always getting their way, but they almost always resent not getting their say. Engle also taught him that part of being a good teacher is sensing when to get off players' backs, when to say, "Let's knock off today and have some laughs, and tomorrow we'll start all over again—from a higher plateau" (Paterno & Asbell, 1989, p. 84).

Eventually, through trial and error, Paterno discovered that there were different ways to handle different people. He remembered saying to Rip Engle that he could not understand how one player could have such a different outlook on football from another player, even though they both came from the same high school and the same football program. How could one be so gung-ho to practice while the other couldn't get himself out of first gear? Engle said, "Joe, the longer you're in this business, the more you're going to realize that everybody's different" (Paterno & Asbell, 1989, p. 84). But Paterno still had trouble understanding this until he had his own family. Then, he saw for himself: same home, same parents, different outcomes. So Paterno learned what Vince Lombardi always preached. Coaches who can outline plays on a blackboard are a dime a dozen. The ones who win "get inside their players and motivate them" (Paterno & Asbell, 1989, p. 92).

It did not take Paterno long to see the results of the astute application of human resource leadership behavior. By 1971 and 1972, he began to see more clearly, more specifically, how an emerging Penn State style of football was enriching his players far beyond winning and losing. It had to do with pride; it had to do with caring about their teammates as people, as a community. It had to do with love. The difference is difficult to put into words, but just before every game, he has a need to touch each player—physically touch him. He needs to do it to assure each player that he knows how hard he has worked and that the game and its outcome belongs to all of them collectively.

In this light, Paterno observes that to some coaches, graduation is a disaster, the enemy. That's when they lose all of their good players. However, with Paterno, all the things he believes in force him to celebrate graduation as an achievement, as a victory.

Paterno recalls a number of situations in which the effective use of human resource behavior made a difference. Paterno started Mike Cooper as the first black quarterback in Penn State history. When he received complaints and threats from some of the alumni, he decided to "make a statement" by starting Charlie Pittman, Franco Harris, Lydell Mitchell, and Mike Cooper, all African Americans, in the backfield all at the same time.

In another instance, Paterno faulted himself for not using human resource behavior when it was appropriate. It seems that Franco Harris was three minutes late for practice one day. Paterno reamed him out in front of the team. Afterward, Paterno felt that he had mishandled the situation. In retrospect, instead of popping off in front of the team, which he felt Harris had offended, he wished he had held his peace, spoken to Harris privately later, and tried to determine what was bothering him.

Paterno knows he did something right when he recalls John Cappelletti's acceptance speech upon receiving the Heisman Trophy as the best college football player. Upon receiving the trophy, Cappelletti said that he would like to dedicate it to the many who had touched his life and helped him, but especially to the youngest member of his family, Joseph, who was very ill. He had leukemia. If he could dedicate the trophy to Joseph that night and give him a couple of days of happiness, it would mean the world to John. For John, it was a "battle" on a field but only in the fall. For Joseph, it was all year round. Cappelletti said that the Heisman was more his brother's than his "because of the inspiration" his brother had been to him.

Bishop Fulton J. Sheen was on the dais that night. When he got up to give the benediction, he said, "Maybe for the first time in your lives you have heard a speech from the heart and not from the lips. Part of John's triumph was made by Joseph's sorrow. You don't need a blessing. God had already blessed you in John Cappelletti." And what was Joe Paterno's reaction to all this? "Do you see now why I could never leave for a professional coaching job?" (Paterno & Asbell, 1989, p. 172).

Yet another example of the benefits of Paterno's continuous use of human resource leadership behavior in his football program was the celebration after his first national championship at Penn State. He and his team went on a whistle-stop tour of Pennsylvania on a railroad train. The towns along the way sent out their fire engines to greet the team. With emergency lights circling, each town's engines escorted the team up the highway to deliver them into the care of the next town's engines on a hundred-mile relay of joy and pride. In Paterno's own words, "I never saw such love between people who didn't even know each other" (Paterno & Asbell, 1989, p. 232).

THE SYMBOLIC FRAME

In the symbolic frame, the organization is seen as a stage, a theater in which every actor plays certain roles, and the symbolic leaders attempt to communicate the right impressions to the right audiences. Like most of his coaching colleagues, Joe Paterno makes frequent use of symbolic frame leadership behavior. From his insistence on understated uniforms with no names on the back or logos on the helmets, to reinforce Penn State's "team" approach, to his attire on the sidelines, Paterno is a master at getting his points across symbolically. As a result, Paterno is one of the most respected, beloved, and certainly most recognizable college football coaches in America. Patrolling the sidelines in signature dark glasses and a tie during a game, he dares to wear his trousers rolled up, with white athletic socks and football cleats helping to define the differences between his football program and others. In adopting his philosophy, Paterno harkens back to his high school literary hero, Aeneas. "A hero of Aeneas's kind does not wear his name on the back of his uniform. He doesn't wear Nittany Lions on his helmet to claim star credit for touchdowns and tackles that were enabled by everybody else doing his job" (Paterno & Asbell, 1989, p. 46).

In a not-so-veiled critique of another prominent football program, Paterno once recalled how at Brown the football players weren't ordered to lock themselves away in a deluxe, carpeted athletic dorm like the one Bear Bryant built at Alabama. He speculates that Bryant might have believed in protecting his Red Tide from the mental distractions of a university. In Paterno's opinion, Bryant sheltered his squad of stars from the students who didn't play serious football. Paterno thanks God that he wasn't "protected" in that way at Brown, and at Penn State he wouldn't for one minute think of segregating his players from the rest of the student body. Paterno wants his players to discover themselves—by discovering all the different kinds of people they will encounter among the thirty-seven thousand students at Penn State. According to him, the purpose of college football is to serve education, not the other way around. He called it his "Grand Experiment."

When Paterno is asked to name the best team that he ever coached, he alludes to a quote from Knute Rockne: "I'll find out what my best team is when I find out how many doctors and lawyers, good husbands, and good citizens have come off of each and every one of my teams" (Paterno & Asbell, 1989, p. 17). Like every coach, Paterno loves winning games. But while committing everything they've got to playing their very best game, his players have been coached to know that there's something that counts more than winning.

Paterno recalls receiving a letter of recommendation from Libby McKinney, an English teacher from Pineville, West Virginia. The teacher wrote about a boy whom she taught and how she was impressed by his "natural brightness." She urged Paterno to look at his football talents for a scholarship to Penn State, where she knew athletics would not be permitted to overshadow his education. The student/athlete turned out to be Kurt Warner, one of the most prolific running backs in Penn State football history.

Paterno used symbols in communicating his football philosophy to his players and the broader public. For example, it is common practice among football coaches to use aggressive terms in describing players' roles. A "blood end" was a defensive man who lined up in a certain way. A "monster back" was a secondary player playing the field. Paterno, in his own inimitable style, renamed these terms. For example, he renamed the monster back the "hero back."

This symbolic behavior has helped Paterno define the meaning of the chant "We are Penn State." To his players, the students, and the alums, those words remind them of the special symbols associated with Penn State: those black shoes, those plain uniforms with no glitter and no names. A Penn State player doesn't have to let the whole world know, by putting six Nittany Lions on his helmet, that he has made six big plays. When he scores a touchdown, he doesn't dance and go berserk in the end zone. When a Penn Stater goes on that field, he *expects* to score a touchdown.

Finally, Joe Paterno shows his respect and gratitude to Penn State symbolically. He and his wife are renowned for their charitable contributions to academics at Penn State. They have contributed over $4 million toward various departments and colleges, including support for the Pasquerilla Spiritual Center, which opened in 2003, and the Penn State All-Sports Museum, which opened in 2002. As mentioned in his background, after helping raise over $13 million in funds for the Pattee Library, the university named the expansion in his honor. In Joe Paterno's mind, however, his gifts are "peanuts" compared to the benefits that he and his family have received from Penn State. "Three of our kids have graduated from Penn State" (Paterno & Asbell, 1989, p. 205). Enough said.

THE POLITICAL FRAME

Leaders operating out of the political frame clarify what they want and what they can get. Political leaders are realists above all. They never let what they want cloud their judgment about what is possible. They assess the distribution of power and interests. Paterno is one of the more astute college football coaches in using political frame leadership behavior.

In 2002, Paterno saw Tony Johnson catch a pass for a first down with both feet in bounds on the stadium's video replay board, but the play was ruled an incompletion. Penn State had rallied from a 35–13 deficit with nine minutes left in the game to tie the score at 35, and they were driving on their first possession in overtime for a touchdown to tie the game at 42. Penn State failed on the fourth down, and Iowa held on for the win. Just weeks later, in the final minute of the Michigan game, the same wide receiver, Johnson, made a catch, which would have given Penn State a first down and put them in range for a game-winning field goal. Although Johnson was ruled out of bounds, replays clearly showed that he had both feet in bounds, making the catch legal. Paterno used these two instances to reinforce his longtime efforts to engage instant replay in college football.

In 2003, the Big Ten Conference became the first college football conference to adopt a form of instant replay. The previous two incidents, along with Paterno's public objection and statements, are often cited as catalysts for its adoption. Within the next year, almost all of the Division I-A conferences had adopted a form of instant replay.

Paterno used political leadership behavior to impact a number of other college football issues. He has long advocated for some type of college football play-off system. The question has been posed to him frequently over the years, as only one of his five undefeated teams has been voted national champions. The awarding of the national championship to the team that wins the designated bowl game in a particular year was instituted largely because of Paterno's insistence on a play-off system.

Paterno also believes that scholarship college athletes should receive a modest stipend so that they have some spending money. As justification, he points out that many scholarship athletes are from poor families and that other students have time to hold down a part-time job. On the other hand, busy practice and conditioning schedules prevent college athletes from working during the school year. He constantly uses his influence with the NCEA to promote this view.

Paterno often used his numerous professional coaching offers to his political advantage. He was once wooed by the New England Patriots and seriously considered leaving Penn State, even announcing his acceptance of the position only to change his mind suddenly the next day. This sudden switch in decision had at least two happy results. Later in the morning, after the news conference announcing that he would stay at Penn State, his athletic director, Bob Paterson, called and "ordered" Paterno to fly with him immediately to Pittsburgh to see a lawyer. Penn State didn't want any more close calls. That day, they agreed to the first formal contract that Paterno and Penn State had ever had. The other happy result had to do with his good friend, former Oklahoma coach Chuck Fairbanks, who got the Patriot job that he turned down.

In another instance of Paterno's using political frame leadership behavior, he recalls the time when Tommy Prothro of UCLA beat Penn State 49–11. With only two minutes left in the game and with this huge lead, Prothro called for an on-sides kick as a surprise tactic to recover the ball for an additional score. After the game, reporters asked Paterno what he thought of the maneuver. Even though he was fuming, he decided to utilize some political behavior and said, "Oh no! I think Coach Prothro had something he wanted to try out with this team" (Paterno & Asbell, 1989, p. 92).

Paterno's attitude is that if political leadership behavior can accomplish something good for his team, so be it. If a team needs new facilities as a condition for success and the coach has the power to get them, according to Paterno, he needs to use it. He patterns his use of political behavior after that of Bear Bryant. According to Paterno, Bryant could get summer jobs for his players with just a phone call because he had established many flattering, accommodating relationships. What he put to work was not raw power but a personal charm that made people want to do as he asked.

Former president Richard Nixon was once the recipient of Paterno's political frame behavior. In 1969, when Penn State was undefeated and vying with Alabama for the national championship, Nixon had been quoted as agreeing with the pollsters that Alabama was the best team in the country that year and deserved the national championship. Several years later as a Penn State graduation speaker, Paterno seized the opportunity to get back at Nixon. "How come," he wondered, "a president who knew so much about college football in 1969 could have known so little about Watergate in 1973?" (Paterno & Asbell, 1989, p. 166).

After Paterno's team won its first national championship, he spoke to the university's Board of Trustees. He advised them to stop complaining about the state's not supporting the university and to use the recent success to lobby the lawmakers for more state aid, once again demonstrating Paterno's penchant for using political frame leadership behavior to his and his university's benefit.

Paterno learned to use his political leverage in negotiating his salary at Penn State. When Jackie Sherrill was lured away from Pittsburgh with a huge contract to coach Texas, the senior vice president at Penn State, Steve Garban, was nervous that Paterno would be lured away by a big contract. He asked Paterno if Penn State was paying him enough. Paterno used the opportunity to say, "I don't know. Find out what Bo Schembechler is making at Michigan" (Paterno & Asbell, 1989, p. 249). Paterno got himself an instant $25,000 raise.

CONCLUSION

Joe Paterno's enduring success in college football is no accident. He has sustained his reputation as one of college football's most revered coaches largely because he can astutely adapt his leadership behavior to the ever-changing situation. He could be described as the poster child for the effectiveness of situational leadership theory.

He engages in structural frame leadership behavior by always being well organized, disciplined, and prepared. Additionally, although sometimes wrongly criticized for not doing so, he has adapted his structural behavior to changing situations and times. His offense, for example, is not static but dynamic and varies according to the personnel available.

Paterno's use of human resource frame leadership behavior is well documented. His former players are very loyal to him and recognize that he is sincerely concerned with their well-being long after they graduate—which, unlike players in many big-time college football programs, they almost always do.

Symbolically, Paterno consciously projects the image of a coach who is competent at his craft, cares about the individuals entrusted to his care, and insists on their obtaining a good education to go along with their athletic prowess. We documented a number of instances in which Paterno nurtured this image, including his donation of several million dollars to the Penn State Library.

Finally, we saw how Paterno is not at all shy about using his political clout when necessary. Whether it be with president of the United States, the NCEA, the media, or the Penn State Board of Trustees, Paterno will use whatever leverage he has to be a more effective leader. Joe Paterno is what some have described as "the complete package."

⓫

DON SHULA

Success is not forever and failure isn't fatal.

—Don Shula

BACKGROUND

Born in 1930, Don Shula is best known as the former football coach of
the Miami Dolphins, which he led to an undefeated season and two Super Bowl victories. He currently holds the NFL record for most career
wins with 347.

He graduated from Harvey High School in Painesville, Ohio and from
John Carroll University in Cleveland. He played football at both schools.
He later played with the old Baltimore Colts for four seasons under
Weeb Ewbank before finishing his playing career with the Washington
Redskins.

After his playing career ended, Shula took a position as an assistant
coach at the University of Kentucky in 1959, coaching defensive backs
under head coach Blanton Collier, who would go on to coach the Cincinnati Bengals in the NFL. In 1960, Shula received his first NFL job
as a defensive coordinator for the Detroit Lions.

After Weeb Ewbank left the Baltimore Colts to coach the New York Jets in 1963, Shula was hired by Colts owner Carroll Rosenbloom to coach Baltimore. He was only thirty-three years old. He was very successful, compiling a 71–23–4 record in seven seasons with Baltimore, but he was just 2–3 in the postseason, including two losses in championship games in which the Colts were heavy favorites. He was on the losing side of Super Bowl III, the game in which Joe Namath of the New York Jets guaranteed and delivered a victory. After a string of heartbreaking defeats in the postseason, the 1965 team lost a special tiebreaker playoff game in overtime against the Green Bay Packers while using running back Tom Matte at quarterback because of injuries to John Unitas and his backups. His 1967 team failed to make the play-offs despite a regular season record of 11–1–2.

In 1969, Joe Robbie, owner of the expansion Miami Dolphins, signed Shula to a contract to become Miami's second head coach. As a result of Shula's signing, the team was charged with tampering by the NFL, which forced the Dolphins to give their first-round draft pick to the Colts. It was at Miami that Shula made his mark in the NFL.

Shula's Miami teams were highly successful during the 1970s. They were known for great offensive lines, strong running games, solid quarterbacking, excellent receivers, and a defense that worked well as a cohesive unit. In an era when defenses were given catchy nicknames (for example, the Dallas Cowboys were known as the "Doomsday Defense," Pittsburgh was called "the Steel Curtain," and the Los Angeles Rams' front line was known as "the Fearsome Foursome"), the Dolphins were known as "the No-Name Defense," even though they had a number of great players. In 1972 the Dolphins were unbeaten (14–0) in the regular season. They swept the play-offs and finished the season with a history-making 17–0 record.

Shula was known for his ability to alter his coaching strategy as his personnel changed. His Super Bowl teams in 1971 to 1973 and 1982 were keyed by a run-first offensive strategy and a dominating defense. In 1983, shortly after losing Super Bowl XVII to the Washington Redskins, the Dolphins drafted quarterback Dan Marino out of the University of Pittsburgh. With the talented Marino at quarterback, Shula changed his offensive strategy to feature the passing game. By 1984 the Dolphins were back in the Super Bowl, thanks largely to Marino's record-breaking performances.

The Dolphins' January 1974 Super Bowl win over the Minnesota Vikings proved to be his last championship. Despite consistent success in the regular season, Shula was unable to win in the postseason, failing in twelve trips to the play-offs, including two more Super Bowl appearances, before retiring after the 1995 season.

Shula set numerous records in his thirty-three seasons as a head coach, and he was inducted into the Pro Football Hall of Fame in 1997 (La Morte & Shook, 2004; Shula & Blanchard, 1995; Wikipedia.org).

SITUATIONAL LEADERSHIP ANALYSIS

Situational models of leadership differ from earlier trait and behavioral models in asserting that no single way of leading works in all situations. Rather, appropriate behavior depends on the circumstances at a given time. Effective managers diagnose the situation, identify the leadership style or behavior that will be most effective, and then determine whether they can implement the required style.

Don Shula has worked and published with Ken Blanchard, one of the pioneers of situational leadership theory (see chapter 1). Thus, it is not surprising to find that Shula is a great proponent of situational leadership and adeptly adapts his leadership behavior to the various situations he encounters. Being a disciple of Blanchard's, Shula uses the term *audible-ready* to reflect his belief in "adaptability." Shula doesn't believe in holding to a game plan that isn't working. The key to being adaptable is to be well prepared in the first place. "Audibles" are well thought out and choreographed ahead of time. Shula is always asking, What if? so that when a change occurs, neither he nor his players are caught flat-footed. According to Shula, a fixed game plan or published organizational chart can be deadly to organizations in today's constantly changing environments.

Mercury Morris, one of Shula's star players, pointed out how Shula masterfully adapts his leadership behavior to the situation. In 1970, two years after Martin Luther King Jr.'s assassination, Shula brought in Afro Sheen and Afro combs and put them in the locker room right alongside the Vitalis and Brylcreem. According to Morris, he was trying to relate. It was a sincere gesture. Shula had the ability to adjust to the times and to the people who represented those times. Here's a guy who used to have a rule that you couldn't have a beard. "Now, he's got Louis Oliver, who wears two earrings just a little smaller than basketball hoops," says Morris (Shula & Blanchard, 1995, p. 111).

In another example of Shula's awareness of the situational nature of leadership behavior, he tries to fit his feedback to a player's personality. Bob Griese, his great quarterback in the 1970s, was a very quiet, thoughtful person. He did not respond well to emotional reprimands. On the other hand, Dan Marino, his more recent star quarterback, was a more emotional player and had to be treated in a completely different way. As Mel Phillips, Shula's former defensive backs coach said of him, "Don is sometimes tougher on the team when they win than when they lose. He knows that the team is stronger when we've won and that when we lose, they're already feeling bad enough" (Shula & Blanchard, 1995, p. 102).

THE STRUCTURAL FRAME

Structural leaders seek to develop a new model of the relationship between structure, strategy, and environment in their organizations. Strategic planning, extensive preparation, and effecting change are priorities for them. Don Shula's image is that of a coach squarely placed in the structural leadership mold. The media described both his Baltimore Colts and Miami Dolphin teams as well-oiled machines. In typical structural leadership fashion, Shula focuses on structure, plans, preparation, data, and logic in shaping his programs.

Ever the structural leader, Shula believes that in the end, whether it's sports, business, or education, winning or losing doesn't depend on trick plays or using new systems each week. The information your competition has is not that different from what you have. So what is the key to success and winning? According to Shula, success comes down to a matter of motivating people to work hard and preparing them to play as a team.

Again, from the moment he started coaching professional football in 1963, his day-to-day plan was very specific. He wanted to make sure the team came out of every meeting a little more intelligent than when it went in and left the practice field a little better prepared mentally and physically to play the game than before it arrived. This is all structural frame thinking.

Shula believes that the willingness to create practice systems and procedures aligned with his vision of perfection has produced winning football teams for him over the years: "We want to win them all," he says. "Everything I do is to prepare people to perform to the best of their ability" (Shula & Blanchard, 1995, p. 19). Setting goals is important, but Shula suspects that most organizations overemphasize this process and don't pay enough attention to what needs to be done to accomplish those goals. For example, everybody in the NFL has the goal to reach the play-offs, but not everybody is willing to prepare and do the other things necessary to reach that goal. This is where Shula believes that "overlearning" comes in—repetition to the point that the behavior becomes reflexive.

To Shula, preparation means everything. "I'm passionate about my players being ready for anything" he says. "I see myself as a battlefield commander who has the guts to make the right moves to win. I want to be prepared with a plan and then to expect the unexpected and be ready to change this plan" (Shula & Blanchard, 1995, p. 108). Even the slightest deviation from perfection needs to be corrected on the spot, according to Shula. Correcting and redirecting performance is strategically important—it's where his teams take the measure of the competition.

Along these lines, Shula thinks that the great majority of leaders want to be popular, but he never cared about that. He wanted to be respected. Respect is different from popularity. You can't make it happen or demand it from people, although, according to Shula, some leaders try to. You can only get respect, as has often been pointed out, by earning it.

Shula's structural frame way of thinking transcends even family ties. In 1994 his Miami Dolphins played against the Cincinnati Bengals, coached by his son David. His wife, Mary Anne, was the only member of the family rooting for the Dolphins. Shula's children all felt that David needed the victory more than their dad did. In Shula's heart, he might have agreed, but his responsibility was to his team. He wanted to see David win, and win a lot. "I just didn't want to see him win that Sunday," he said (Shula & Blanchard, 1995, p. 100).

Shula agrees with his organizational development mentor, Ken Blanchard, that many people have the wrong idea about consistency. They think it means behaving the same way all the time. Shula and Blanchard believe that if you praise people and are nice to them when they're performing well and also when they are behaving poorly, that's inconsistent. Consistency is behaving the same way under similar circumstances. "Effective coaches and leaders confront their people, praise them sincerely, redirect or reprimand them without apology, and above all, are honest with them," says Shula (Shula & Blanchard, 1995, p. 156).

However, as with any of the leadership frames, one can overuse structural frame leadership behavior. Shula is fond of recalling the time when he saw someone he didn't recognize in the Dolphins locker room before a game. "Who the hell is that?" he asked.

"He's a writer."

"Get him out of here," said Shula. With that, author and consummate gentleman James Michener left the Dolphins locker room (Shula & Blanchard, 1995, p. 102).

THE HUMAN RESOURCE FRAME

Human resource leaders believe in people and communicate that belief. They are passionate about *productivity through people*. Although Don Shula may seem fixated on winning and is keen on structural leadership behaviors, such as intense game preparation and a disciplined attention to detail, he definitely displays a human side. Tommy Watson, the Dolphin's long-time home-game pastor, recalls seeing this human side of Shula at the birth of his grandson. Watson noticed a concerned look on Shula's face before a game and thought that it might be because of two straight defeats. Shula told him, upon being questioned, "Oh no, Tommy. That's not on my mind. My son David's wife is in the hospital right now, about to give birth" (Shula & Blanchard, 1995, p. 44).

According to Ken Blanchard, Shula's friend and mentor, most football fans are familiar with Shula's jutting jaw and determined scowl as he strides up and down the sidelines, but probably few know his soft, gentle, and vulnerable side. "It's the side of the man that keeps his ego under control," says Blanchard (Shula & Blanchard, 1995, p. 47).

The relationship that Shula wants to establish with his followers is one not of fear but of mutual respect. He wants his players to respect him for giving them everything he has to prepare them to play the best that they can play. His respect for them comes from knowing that they are willing to give him all that they have to prepare themselves to play. Shula believes that the same things that make you successful as a coach make you successful as a father or a husband. He hopes that people respect him for the way he runs his personal life as well as the way he coaches the Miami Dolphins.

According to Shula, one of the ways leaders can earn respect is by admitting when they've made mistakes. For example, in a game with the Jets, behind by three with three minutes left with a fourth and five, he decided to punt. Dan Marino objected, thinking the Dolphins would never get the ball back. However, they did and won. But if they had not won, Shula said, he would have personally accepted responsibility "rather than blaming it on poor execution or something else" (Shula & Blanchard, 1995, p. 52).

As one of Shula's assistant coaches, Joe Greene, testified to Shula's use of human resource frame leadership behavior. "He wants you to know everything about the players for whom you're responsible—how much they weigh, what they're thinking" (Shula & Blanchard, 1995, p. 62). Some of it may look like babysitting, but Shula insists that everyone who works with him be totally involved, and that includes knowing what is happening in the players' lives outside of football.

In another incident evincing Shula's human resource touch, he made a hospital visit to Mike Westhoff, his special teams coach, who had been diagnosed with bone cancer. Shula asked him how he was doing and, hearing that he was doing okay, went on to tell Westhoff how much he needed him to be ready by training camp in July because "we're going all the way this year." Westhoff said, "I thought he would tuck me in, but he didn't. He treated me the way I *could be*, not the way I *was*" (Shula & Blanchard, 1995, p. 73).

Shula believes that practicing human resource behavior is essential in recognizing good performance. The Miami blitz is on. A defensive tackle breaks through the offensive line and nails the quarterback for an eight-yard loss. Shula is the first one to greet the tackle as he comes off the field. "Nice job," he exclaims. It is his practice to recognize his players in front of their peers. His coaches and he will stop and give a player a pat on the back or recognize a great team effort on the spot, but they usually continue the feedback at a team meeting to give the players even fuller recognition.

After he had been coaching for a few years, he got into the pattern of starting a team meeting by recognizing the less-publicized players. Like most NFL teams, the day after a game, the coaches hold a meeting to review the players' performances. The entire squad views the game films, but Shula focuses on the often neglected special teams. Shula uses this time to create opportunities for players to appreciate each other's efforts. In doing so, Shula practices one of Ken Blanchard's leadership principles of "catching people doing something *right*."

Along these lines, when Shula gets upset with a player or the team, he always focuses on *performance*. Respect for his players is a given. He's sometimes tough on his players, but they know that he respects them as human beings. Shula admittedly wears his feelings on his sleeve. But he is honest and straight with people, and he expects them to be the same way with him.

THE SYMBOLIC FRAME

In the symbolic frame, the organization is seen as a stage, a theater in which every actor plays certain roles, and the symbolic leader attempts to communicate the right impressions to the right audiences. Like many of his counterparts in the coaching profession, Don Shula frequently utilizes symbolic frame leadership behavior.

An example is the acronym he uses to express his coaching philosophy, "COACH to Win" (Shula & Blanchard, 1995, p. 21):

Conviction driven: Effective leaders stand for something.
Overlearning: Effective leaders help their teams achieve practice perfection.
Audible ready: Effective leaders prepare their teams to change as the situation demands.
Consistency: Effective leaders are predictable in their response to performance.
Honesty based: Effective leaders are high integrity and clear and straightforward in their interactions with others.

In typical symbolic leadership behavior style, Shula believes the problem with most leaders today is that they don't stand for anything. Leadership implies movement toward something, and convictions provide that direction, according to Shula. "If you don't stand for something, you'll fall for anything," he says (Shula & Blanchard, 1995, p. 27). Shula believes that in the long run, winning coaching has more to do with the coach's own beliefs. To be an effective coach, one may have to set aside temporarily his fascination with the science of the game and look first at what's true for himself.

The realization of a dream like the Dolphin's 1972 unbeaten season is invariably the result of a strong set of operating beliefs and principles that are continually in evidence throughout the formation, training, and day-to-day practice of a team. Shula always reflects a set of core beliefs, values, and convictions that support his vision of perfection:

- Keep winning and losing in perspective.
- Lead by example.
- Go for respect over popularity.
- Value character as well as ability.
- Work hard but enjoy what you do (Shula & Blanchard, 1995, p. 29).

Shula often uses his religious beliefs as a manifestation of symbolic leadership behavior. Attending Mass and looking to God for guidance aren't just perfunctory acts to Shula. To him, they matter deeply, especially when he is in his world of shrill whistles and crashing bodies. And when game day comes, these beliefs keep things in perspective for him. His faith tells him that success is not forever, and failure isn't fatal. It makes a real difference to him that he starts each day giving thanks and asking help from God. His son David noticed Shula's devotion to God in the fact that he didn't lose faith. He didn't give up, and he didn't quit. And the reason that he didn't was because he had confidence that someone was watching over him.

True to symbolic frame leadership behavior, Shula doesn't know any other way to lead but by example. His example is in things like his high standards of performance, his attention to detail, and—above all—hard work. He once had an Achilles tendon operation on a Friday and returned to coach a game on Sunday. He sums up his attitude toward work as follows: "To be successful, all you have to do is work half-days; you can work the first twelve hours or the second twelve hours." Shula is also fond of quoting Confucius: "Choose work you love, and you will never have to work a day in your life."

As another indication of his penchant for using symbolic leadership behavior, he harkens back to a tradition that he had for his 1972 Super Bowl team. They sprinted to the other end of the field at the end of the third quarter, when everyone else usually was dragging. He always had a hunch that not every Dolphin felt like running, but when a guy saw his captain, Keith Byars, doing it, the enthusiasm often rubbed off.

Finally, Shula projects the symbolic image of someone whose integrity is beyond reproach. He was a member of the NFL Rules Committee for many years. According to him, doing something unethical or dishonest would erode his self-esteem—his image of who he was as a person. He espouses the ideology of T. Kerr, former chairman of Chevron Corporation, who said, "There's no doubt in my mind that being ethical pays, because I know that, in our company, people who sleep well at night work better in the day" (Shula & Blanchard, 1995, p. 154).

THE POLITICAL FRAME

Leaders operating out of the political frame clarify what they want and what they can get. Political leaders are realists above all. They never let what they want cloud their judgment about what is possible. They assess the distribution of power and interests. Don Shula is known to use political leadership behavior when appropriate. He was often accused of using his membership on the Rules Committee to establish rules that would be to his and his team's best advantage. For example, he had the rules tightened for protecting the quarterback when he had Dan Marino playing for him.

In 2007 Shula made a public comment alluding to an asterisk being placed on the Patriots if they went undefeated and broke his 1972 Dolphins record, because the spygate controversy (the Patriots were caught filming the opposing team's practices) had caused the NFL to fine the Patriots and take away a first-round draft pick. This was the subject of some controversy because his own hiring by the Miami Dolphins was ruled to be a form of tampering by the NFL and cost the Dolphins a first-round draft pick in 1970. As a result, Shula has since backed off his initial comments.

CONCLUSION

Although his serious nature and appearance, not to mention his disciplined approach to coaching, identify him as a quintessential structural frame leader, Don Shula's leadership behavior manifests all four Bolman-Deal frames of leadership behavior. Granted, his preference for, and comfort level with, structural frame behavior is well documented, but we have seen that he truly cares about people's well-being and is sensitive to their needs—human resource behavior traits.

Like many in his profession, he adeptly uses symbols in transmitting his ideals and values to his followers. We saw how he likes to use slogans and quotations to get his points across and how he models desired behavior. And as far as the use of political frame leadership behavior is concerned, he is not shy about using his position of power in his own and his team's service. He also used his political influence when his first wife, Dorothy, fought breast cancer for six years. Just before her death in 1991, Shula formed the Don Shula Foundation for the purpose of finding a cure for cancer.

Suffice it to say, Don Shula is an effective situational leadership theory practitioner. His close friend Ken Blanchard and a colleague, Paul Hersey, developed their own approach to situational leadership theory as noted in chapter 1. Needless to say, Blanchard's pupil, Don Shula, has earned very high grades and graduated near the top of the class.

12

BILL WALSH

There is only one way to do anything: the right way.

—Golda Meir

BACKGROUND

Born in 1931, Bill Walsh became renowned as the head football coach of the San Francisco 49ers. He also coached at Stanford University and, with both teams, popularized what has become known as the West Coast offense. Walsh's record of achievement with the 49ers included winning ten of his fourteen postseason games, along with six division titles, three NFC Championship titles, and three Super Bowls. For his career, he was 102–63–1. He was named the NFL's coach of the year in 1981 and 1984.

Walsh started his career in football as a running back for Hayward High School in California. After graduating, he went to San Jose State University, where he played as a tight end and a defensive end. Walsh graduated with a bachelor's degree in physical education in 1955. He served under Bob Bronzan as a graduate assistant coach on the Spartans football coaching staff and graduated with a master's degree in physical

education from San Jose State in 1959, thus placing him alongside Joe
Gibbs as the only two coaches profiled here with advanced degrees.

Following graduation from San Jose State, Walsh coached football at
Washington High School in Fremont, California. Walsh then accepted
an assistant coaching position with Marv Levy, who would later become
the coach of the Buffalo Bills, and who had just been hired as the head
coach at the University of California, Berkeley. After coaching at California, he did a stint at Stanford as an assistant coach, before beginning
his professional coaching career.

He began his NFL coaching career in 1966 as an assistant with the
Oakland Raiders. As a Raider assistant, Walsh was mentored in the ver-
tical passing (long passes) offense by Sid Gillman. Walsh would later use
this training to develop a predominantly horizontal passing (short passes)
approach, which came to be known as the "West Coast" offense.

Walsh then moved to the expansion Cincinnati Bengals in 1968,
serving under Paul Brown for seven seasons as one of the architects of
the team's offense. When Brown retired as head coach following the
1975 season and appointed Bill "Tiger" Johnson as his successor, a dis-
gruntled Walsh resigned and moved on to the San Diego Chargers for
the next two years. Next, Walsh was hired as the head coach at Stanford
University, where he stayed for two seasons. His two Stanford teams
went 9–3 in 1977 with a win in the Sun Bowl and 8–4 in 1978 with a win
in the Bluebonnet Bowl.

Following his success at Stanford, Walsh was hired as head coach of
the San Francisco 49ers in 1979. The long-suffering 49ers had a history
of losing seasons before Walsh's arrival. His first season with the 49ers
showed no improvement. However, in 1979, Walsh drafted quarterback
Joe Montana from Notre Dame. Walsh named Montana the starting
quarterback in 1980, and the rest is history. San Francisco won its first
Super Bowl championship in 1981. Under Walsh, the 49ers won Super
Bowl championships again in 1984 and 1988.

In 1988, Walsh left the coaching ranks immediately following his
team's third Super Bowl victory and became a broadcaster for NBC.
Walsh returned to Stanford in 1992 to serve once again as head coach,
leading the Cardinals to a 10–3 record and a Pacific-10 Conference co-
championship. After consecutive losing seasons, Walsh left Stanford in
1994 and retired from coaching.

Walsh returned to the 49ers, serving as vice president and general manager from 1999 to 2001 and acting as special consultant to the team for three years afterwards. In 2004, Walsh was appointed as special assistant to the athletic director at Stanford. Walsh also authored two books, was a motivational speaker, and taught classes at the Stanford Graduate School of Business.

Walsh was diagnosed with leukemia in 2004. He died on July 30, 2007, at his home in Woodside, California. He is enshrined in the Pro Football Hall of Fame (Walsh & Dickey, 1998; Wikipedia .org).

SITUATIONAL LEADERSHIP ANALYSIS

Situational models of leadership differ from earlier trait and behavioral models in asserting that no single way of leading works in all situations. Rather, appropriate behavior depends on the circumstances at a given time. Effective managers diagnose the situation, identify the leadership style or behavior that will be most effective, and then determine whether they can implement the required style.

Although "Professor" Bill Walsh's image is very much in the structural frame leadership style, he very adeptly adapted his leadership behavior to the situation in which he found himself. There is ample evidence that he utilized all four of Bolman-Deal's frames of leadership in different situations. For example, in contrast to previous multiple Super Bowl champions like the Green Bay Packers, the Pittsburgh Steelers, and the current New England Patriots, Walsh kept changing, rebuilding as he was winning, with six divisional championships and seven play-off appearances in his last eight years. Each Super Bowl team was quite different; only five 49ers played in all three Super Bowls, and only three of them played major roles.

His being the first coach to "script" the first twenty-five plays of the game could give one the impression that Walsh was locked into a certain set of behaviors "come hell or high water." Such was not the case, however. If it were, if the 49ers were on the one-yard line after the eighth play, for example, Walsh would automatically call a long pass if that were on the script. Obviously, the system had to be much more flexible than that to be successful. In his own words, he described his flexibility in using different leadership behaviors in different situations. "We were quite willing to go against accepted strategy formula to call a pass when other teams expected a run, or vice versa. That made it more difficult for teams to use special defenses against us" (Walsh, 1990, p. 9).

Other instances of Walsh's adapting his leadership behavior to the situation include the 1970 season, when his starting quarterback was injured, and he picked up Virgil Carter, a very marginal quarterback. With Carter at quarterback, the 49ers won the division with what Walsh described as a "nickel-and-dime offense" (Walsh, 1990, p. 35). As he added talent to the team, however, he broadened his passing game. When Isaac Curtis was drafted, he emphasized passes down the field to take advantage of his great speed. Finally, when Jerry Rice joined the 49ers, they were able to take the passing game to another level.

Finesse can bring success with less than great players. With tactics, skill, and techniques, Walsh found a way to win. In 1981, with a few outstanding individuals surrounded by less gifted players, they succeeded. As the team improved, the techniques continued to develop and they became recognized as among the very best. So, ultimately, the 49ers combined their finesse with power and strength to become the "team of the '80s" (Walsh, 1990, p. 42).

Walsh's players recognized the situational nature of his behavior and the need for such varied behavior in order to succeed. One of his former players said, "As the stylish, graceful, accommodating, easy-going, affable, 'players' coach, he was able to understand us. He let us decide what we needed. That approach will get up to 80 percent of the job done. The final 20 percent can be directly attributed to making tough decisions, demonstrating a high standard of performance, meeting expectations, paying attention to details and grabbing and shaking when necessary" (Walsh, 1990, p. 97).

Walsh observed that a number of coaches become quite prominent and successful in their early years in the NFL, only to disappear when they should be in their prime. According to Walsh, these are the coaches who depend too much on rhetoric, dialogue, and buzz words or on the number of times they have been in the presence of certain people and on the impression they make, instead of expanding their knowledge base, expertise, and skills. This is an instance of a leader using strictly symbolic leadership behavior to the detriment of structural leadership behavior, ultimately resulting in ineffectiveness. Walsh never fell into this trap.

THE STRUCTURAL FRAME

Structural leaders seek to develop a new model of the relationship between structure, strategy, and environment in their organizations. Strategic planning, extensive preparation, and effecting change are priorities for them. Although often described as a "players' coach," which assumes the use of human resource behavior, Bill Walsh was also known for being well prepared, well organized, and disciplined in his approach—all structural frame characteristics.

Walsh developed a checklist for himself of traits that he believed lead to effective leadership. They included

- Be accountable.
- Be a leader.
- Be committed to excellence.
- Be positive.
- Be prepared.
- Be organized.
- Be focused.
- Be ethical.
- Be flexible.

Walsh learned early in his career the need for structural frame leadership behavior. He recalled a loss to the Oakland Raiders in the final seconds early in his career as an assistant coach that had a significant impact on him. He made certain that by the time he joined the 49ers as their head coach, he could account for those critical, almost desperate situations at the end of a game. He devised and practiced a last-second play for that and for every other conceivable situation.

Preplanning in this way means that one doesn't have to depend entirely on spontaneous judgment during the game. Weather can even be a factor, according to Walsh. He remembered days when he had been dizzy from the heat on the sideline in Los Angeles and so cold in Chicago that he could hardly talk. Having a ready list of plays helps counteract that, he indicated.

Famous for developing the so-called West Coast offense, Walsh utilized structural leadership behavior in its development and implementation. In the process, he had taken his team beyond a past pattern of failure and finger-pointing so that the responsibility for the success of an offense started with the coach. The offense was then executed by the players, who were extremely well prepared. He spent hours on everything a quarterback does, every step he takes, how he moves between pass rushers or to the outside, when he goes to alternate receivers—all the details.

In true structural frame form, Walsh made sure that every effort was made to keep a businesslike atmosphere on the sideline, with people thinking as clearly as they could, without becoming either distraught or so pleased that they were celebrating. He had learned this approach from one his mentors, Paul Brown, the legendary coach of the Cleveland Browns and the Cincinnati Bengals. Brown was the epitome of the structural frame leader. He implemented a highly organized and structured format that transformed the game into the modern era. His teams were noted for their almost mechanical, error-free precision, an approach that Walsh openly emulated.

Thus, when Walsh became head coach of the 49ers, he methodically set about structuring the organization by using all the contacts he had made in coaching. Before his first 49ers training camp, he set up the schedule and planned the agenda for the entire camp, accounting for every hour of every day. His first step in developing a plan for the upcoming year would be to hold a series of meetings with his coaching staff, collectively and individually, to discuss the four basic categories of team development: (1) teaching the individual fundamentals and skills; (2) choreographing the action of groups, such as the defensive backs or the offensive linemen; (3) developing team execution; and (4) implementing situational football, as related to game circumstances.

He requested that each coach isolate those fundamentals and skills for his position and prioritize them, then explain and justify the drills required to develop them. He determined that each drill must have a direct relationship to a specific action the player would experience in a game. He never tolerated drills that had no purpose other than taking up time—what teachers often refer to as "make-work." Every logical situation that might occur in a game was isolated, and strategy and tactics were devised accordingly. These situations were given priorities with a specified number of practice minutes devoted to them.

According to Walsh, running a football franchise is not unlike running any other business. You start first with a structural format and basic philosophy, then find the people who can implement it. This typically structural frame mind set dominated his thinking even during the strike year in the NFL, when "replacement" teams were organized to take the place of the striking players. More than most teams, the 49ers worked very hard to be ready when the strike occurred. They established a complete subprogram to secure and develop replacement talent.

Walsh was so organized that he had a plan for everything. For example, he published a list entitled "Prerequisites for Assistant Coaches":

- They must have a complete working knowledge of the game because players respect that above everything else.
- Coaches must be able to effectively implement a program for each player that best develops his individual skills.
- Taking a personal interest in each player is absolutely essential.
- You must have people who can communicate well under the stress of a season, so you need the kind of personality that can work with others.
- The ability to express oneself is vital because a logical, articulate person is best suited for teaching.
- The coaching ethic of commitment and personal sacrifice is the basis of the job (Walsh, 1990, p. 103).

Walsh used the structural leadership approach to avoid complacency and decisions based on emotion rather than reason. According to Walsh, luxury and convenience can bring on complacency, and he "rode everyone hard" to avoid it. He had to become almost computerized to function effectively. In his view, a coach simply cannot afford to indulge in the emotion of the moment. Players have an excess of emotion. They need from the coach decisive direction and stability—both structural frame traits.

Finally, in true structural frame leadership manner, Walsh believed that one of the basic tenets in establishing the organization was to make it so solid that it could survive anyone's departure, including his own. He took great pride in the 49ers' continuing to thrive, winning the Super Bowl the year following his retirement under his successor, George Seifert.

THE HUMAN RESOURCE FRAME

Human resource leaders believe in people and communicate that belief. They are passionate about *productivity through people*. In a number of instances, Bill Walsh acknowledged and practiced human resource frame leadership behavior. He was famous for making some irrelevant remark just to lighten things up in a crucial situation. For example, during the Cincinnati Bengals game in 1984, when Joe Montana came to the sideline after throwing his third interception in the first half, he said, "How's it going out there?" Montana grinned at the remark, seemed to relax, and played much better in the second half (Walsh, 1990, p. 18).

Walsh learned the importance of human resource behavior by observing Paul Brown's failure to use it. I mentioned earlier that Walsh credited Brown with teaching him the importance of structural leadership behavior. However, that was not the case regarding human resource leadership behavior. According to Walsh, Paul Brown was obsessively interested in the development of the Cincinnati Bengals, not in his coaches' careers. He felt team harmony and productivity were more important than personal ambitions. As long as you were dedicated exclusively to his organization, everything was copacetic. But he was self-serving to the point that Walsh believed it had taken him so long to land a head coaching job in the NFL because Brown denigrated him to potential employers so that he would remain with the Bengals. So, as far as human resource behavior is concerned, Walsh looked to one of his other mentors, Tommy Prothro, the former San Diego Chargers coach. Not only was Prothro a great football man, but, as Walsh would say, "his personal ethics and principles set a standard for me in future years" (Walsh, 1990, p. 49).

Walsh used human resource behavior out of enlightened self-interest. He believed that the coaches who have been most successful are usually the ones actively involved in both the on-the-field, day-to-day activities and the off-field activities. He claimed that players will sacrifice more for a hands-on coach because they identify with him as an integral part of the team. He contrasts this with the "administrative" coach who outsources, or delegates, most of his duties.

Communicating on a first-name basis is very appropriate, according to Walsh. He believes that there is very little room for protocol in an atmosphere in which so many sacrifices are made. Insecure men may need the continual reinforcement of being referred to by titles, but players will be much more willing to openly express themselves if formalities are set aside. When a coach starts becoming more of a symbolic leader, instead of being directly involved with coaching, Walsh said, "he'd better start looking for career alternatives," because eventually the result will start appearing on the scoreboard (Walsh, 1990, p. 61).

Along these same lines, Walsh thought a coach should celebrate because of who his players *are*, not because they won another game. Some coaches, under tremendous pressure to win, will compromise everything. Players become objects, and they are manipulated to help the coach survive and to satisfy his personal needs. Walsh, on the other hand, thought coaches should always appreciate the athletes and remind themselves that the game was not designed for the coach to orchestrate but for the athletes to participate.

In another display of human resource behavior, and to introduce more men of color to the game, he helped initiate in 1987 a fellowship program for minority coaches. This program served to identify those coaches with the potential to become part of the NFL as assistant and ultimately head coaches. This model program has since been adopted by the entire NFL. Walsh was also the first coach to assure a full measure of communication between all athletes and coaches, black and white, by hiring Dr. Harry Edwards, civil rights activist and professor of sociology at the University of California, Berkeley, to serve as a counselor and personal consultant.

As each man passed rather quickly through his 49ers career, Walsh felt obligated to prepare him for when it was time to leave professional football. This took careful planning, sensitive timing, and preparation of the athlete for the moment. The 49ers were unique because of the personal interest that both Ed DeBartolo, the owner, and Walsh took in individual players and the team as a whole. They were determined to do what was best for the individuals, even when that did not necessarily benefit the team. For example, during the strike year when the players had no income coming in, although the NFL insisted that they did not get paid, the 49ers found a way to get each player a loan for half of his week's salary.

At the same time that Walsh encouraged human resource behavior, he cautioned that virtue is its own reward. According to Walsh, coaches have to realize that players aren't necessarily going to appreciate what coaches are doing for them. The player assumes that it is part of the coach's job. A coach should practice human resource behavior because it is in the long-term best interest of the athlete and the team. He should not expect anything in return, Walsh pointed out. Given this attitude, we can readily see why Bill Walsh was known as a "players' coach."

THE SYMBOLIC FRAME

In the symbolic frame, the organization is seen as a stage, a theater in which every actor plays certain roles, and the symbolic leader attempts to communicate the right impressions to the right audiences. Bill Walsh was keenly aware of the need for symbolic frame leadership behavior. When he first came to the 49ers, he had known beforehand that he had to change the organization's public image totally. As general manager in 1977 and 1978, Joe Thomas had antagonized almost everybody, which reflected poorly on the owner, Ed DeBartolo, and the organization. Upon assuming the head coaching position, one of the first things that Walsh did was to hire two former players, Ken Flower and R. C. Owens, whose primary responsibility was to change the 49ers image from a bunch of pathetic losers to an organization on the rise.

According to Walsh, everyone in the organization had to be educated in the dynamics of doing business. "I knew we would have a long process of rebuilding," he said, "so we needed the support of everybody" (Walsh, 1990, p. 98). As a result, the 49ers came to be known as a class organization as well as a championship team. They took great pride in playing like a "precision machine." They projected the image of a team not obsessed with individuality and attracting attention. They could thrive in the volatile, sometimes cruel arena of professional football, but do it with class, dignity, and mutual respect.

Walsh often used symbolic leadership to create an "us against them" mentality to motivate his team. When the Los Angeles Rams versus the Dallas Cowboys game was televised rather than the 49ers game, Walsh told the reporters that the 49ers were obviously not accepted nationally because "the jockstrap elitists don't consider us in their comfort zone." There are power sources, influence sources, in the NFL, he claimed. "Forty-five-year-old men who are football groupies who prefer that the 49ers not exist so they can hold onto their football contracts and associations or power groups," he said (Walsh, 1990, p. 139).

Walsh was also adept at telling stories to motivate his teams. On one occasion, he told the story of the British soldiers in Burma during WWII, when the Japanese army seemed unstoppable. The Japanese would capture retreating British soldiers and kill them, making it clear that they were taking no prisoners. Eventually, the British were backed up against a mountain in a small town. It was obvious that they would have to make a stand and fight because there was nowhere to run. They did, and they beat the Japanese back, forcing them to retreat. But they could do that only after they'd been humiliated for so long that they realized they had to fight the Japanese way or be killed. Early on in his 49ers career, Walsh felt that his team was in that same position. They had been humiliated so many times that now it was time to stand up and fight.

He also encouraged his players to exhibit symbolic leadership behavior. Before the 49ers first Super Bowl game, Joe Montana had picked up a song by Kenny Loggins entitled "This Is It." Walsh agreed to have him play it in the locker room before the game because it had a message. One of the lines in the song was, "This is your miracle," which certainly applied to them at the time. As we know, the 49ers went on to win that first Super Bowl. Walsh would not say that playing that song helped win the game, but it sure didn't hurt.

After the 1981 season, when the 49ers surprised everyone by winning a championship, Walsh first started to hear the term *genius* applied to his name. In true symbolic behavior form, he cultivated and encouraged that image. He used it to instill confidence in his team. These examples demonstrate that Bill Walsh used the symbolic frame of leadership behavior very astutely.

THE POLITICAL FRAME

Leaders operating out of the political frame clarify what they want and what they can get. Political leaders are realistic above all. They never let what they want cloud their judgment about what is possible. They assess the distribution of power and interests.

Bill Walsh effectively utilized political frame leadership behavior when appropriate. When Paul Brown stepped down as the founding coach of the Cincinnati Bengals, he named one of his assistant coaches, Bill Johnson, to succeed him. It had been widely believed that Walsh would get the job. Walsh was devastated by the decision, but he was the only one available to speak on the Bengals' behalf for the first forty-eight hours after the announcement. He couldn't refuse interviews; nor could he speak frankly about his disappointment because he certainly didn't want to burden Bill Johnson, who had been a friend for many years. So, he swallowed hard, practiced political leadership behavior, and "took one for the team."

Walsh always stressed "making friends and influencing people." In building the San Francisco 49ers organization, he stressed the importance of not making enemies. He did not want to expend energy on anything but the project at hand. The 49ers couldn't afford an enemy, whether it was NFL coaches and management, league employees, players, the press, college coaches, or fans. He always preached that "one enemy could do more damage than the good done by a hundred friends" (Walsh, 1990, p. 98).

Walsh also liked to use political leadership behavior in resolving conflicts. His formula for resolving conflicts included finding a way to acknowledge something the other person had done, be it a project or decision, outside the original dispute. He also cautioned that we cannot expect to resolve philosophical differences with one conversation. We need to work at it and be sensitive to each person's needs. For example, Lowell Cohn of the *San Francisco Chronicle* wrote a very critical column about Walsh. Instead of overreacting, Walsh made an effort to have a personal conversation with him at their next meeting on an unrelated subject of mutual interest, namely, boxing. In Walsh's view, it was important to keep the lines of communication open and remind each other of their basic mutual respect. They could simply agree to disagree.

Walsh's political frame behavior proved very effective by virtue of the almost universally held opinion that he was a true gentleman.

CONCLUSION

Bill Walsh was keenly aware of the need to adapt one's leadership style to the situation and of the fact that one size doesn't fit all. An article he wrote for the February 26, 1996, edition of *Forbes Magazine* is entitled "What Price Glory? Walking the Line between Ruthless and Toothless." The title implies an effective leader's need to be able to alter his behavior to include autocratic and democratic leadership behaviors and everything in between. Balancing the four frames of leadership behavior is noble in theory but often maddening when one faces the challenges of competitive life, according to Walsh. But he believed that whether one is a general, a CEO, or a football coach, finding the middle ground between the well-being of the people who work for you and the achievement of a goal is one of the trickiest aspects of leadership. While there is no one definitive solution—situations vary from one day to the next—some kind of personal standard on the question of people versus success is imperative. "This applies not just to managers but to the managers of managers," he said (Walsh, 1990, p. 98).

Bill Walsh's success was no mistake. He was the epitome of a situational leader in the Bolman-Deal mold. He effectively utilized all four frames of leadership behavior suggested by their model of situational leadership theory. Additionally, he utilized the four frames in the appropriate circumstances. He was especially adept at behaving out of the structural and human resource frames. Leaders and aspiring leaders can learn much from studying Bill Walsh's leadership style and applying it to their own particular situations.

⓭

LEADERSHIP LESSONS LEARNED

The greatest discovery of my generation is that man can alter his life simply by altering his attitude of mind.

—William James

INTRODUCTION

What do we learn about leadership from these ten remarkably similar coaches? First, we learn that situational leadership theory makes eminent sense. Virtually all of these coaches are effective as leaders because they are able to adapt their leadership behavior to changing situations. None of them is "stuck" in one paradigm. Some, like Bear Bryant, Bill Belichick (structural), and Tony Dungy (human resource), might be criticized for using one or another leadership frame too exclusively, but the reality is that, by and large, they are successful because, to a person, they balance their use of the four leadership frames enunciated by Lee Bolman and Terrence Deal very effectively.

More specifically, we have learned that there are four requisites for effective leadership:

1. a *knowledge* of, and *passion* for, one's field (competency),
2. an ability to engender mutual *trust and respect* with one's followers,
3. a knowledge of the organizational *culture* (readiness level) of one's followers, and
4. an ability to apply *situational leadership theory* to one's practice.

LEADING WITH MIND

Knowledge of one's field is a sine qua non for effective leadership. This quality usually manifests itself in one's structural frame leadership behavior. In football terms, the leader must have a good command of the Xs and Os. In business terms, the effective leader must have at least an adequate knowledge of the technical aspects of how a business operates and a sense of how to develop a business plan. In education, the leader needs to know how schools and school systems operate and what the best practices in the field are in curriculum and instruction. In a family situation, the leader (parent or guardian) needs to have at least a modicum of knowledge regarding the principles of child psychology to be effective. In short, leaders in any field need to know that field and be able to apply that knowledge through the theory and practice of organizational development, which would include the following:

- *Organizational structure:* how an institution is organized
- *Organizational culture:* the values and beliefs of an institution
- *Motivation:* the system of rewards and incentives provided
- *Communication:* the clarity and accuracy of the communication process
- *Decision making:* how and by whom decisions are made
- *Conflict management:* how dysfunctional conflict is handled
- *Power distribution:* how the power in an institution is distributed
- *Strategic planning:* how the mission, vision, and strategic plan are developed
- *Change:* how change is effectively implemented in an institution

I will not go into detail about these processes here. If the reader is interested in a comprehensive look at these processes, I would recommend an earlier publication of mine, *Educational Administration: Leading with Mind and Heart*, second edition. However, I have included at the end of this chapter "The Heart Smart Survey," which I developed to help leaders assess their institution's organizational health and to identify which of the factors listed above are in need of improvement.

LEADING WITH HEART

To recap, then, the effective leader needs to be *technically* competent. However, being technically competent is not enough. To be truly effective, leaders need to master the *art* of leadership and learn to lead with *heart*. In effect, leaders need to operate out of both the structural and political frames (science) and the human resource and symbolic frames (art) to maximize their effectiveness. This means that they must be concerned about the person (*cura personalis*). They must abide by the Golden Rule and treat others as they wish to be treated. As noted in chapter 2, truly effective leaders treat their employees like volunteers and empower them to actualize their true potential, thereby engendering mutual trust and respect among virtually all of their colleagues.

In their new book entitled *Leading with Kindness*, William Baker and Michael O'Malley reiterate my views. They explore how one of the most unheralded features of leadership—basic human kindness—drives successful organizations. And while most scholars generally recognized that a leader's emotional intelligence factors into that person's leadership behavior, most are reticent to consider it as important as analytical ability, decision-making skills, or implementation skills. Such qualities as compassion, empathy, and kindness are often dismissed as unquantifiable and seen as weaknesses. Yet, research in neuroscience and the social sciences clearly reveals that one's physiological and emotional states have measurable effects on both individual and group performance.

In the jargon of the day, individuals who lead with heart or kindness are said to have a high degree of emotional intelligence. Most of us are familiar with the current notion of multiple intelligences; that is, individuals have a number of intelligences in addition to cognitive intelligence. Among these intelligences is emotional intelligence. Several theories within the emotional intelligence paradigm seek to understand how individuals perceive, understand, utilize, and manage emotions in an effort to predict and foster personal effectiveness. Most of these models define emotional intelligence as an array of traits and abilities related to emotional and social knowledge that influence our overall ability to cope effectively with environmental demands; as such, it can be viewed as a model of psychological well-being and adaptation. This includes the ability to be aware of, understand, and relate to others; the ability to deal with strong emotions and control one's impulses; and the ability to adapt to change and solve problems of a personal and social nature. The five main domains of these models are intrapersonal skills, interpersonal skills, adaptability, stress management, and general mood. If the reader sees a similarity between emotional intelligence and what I term *leading with heart* and what Baker and O'Malley call *leading with kindness*, it is not coincidental—it is intentional.

LEADING WITH MIND AND HEART

So, the truly effective leaders lead with *both* mind (science) and heart (art)—with cognitive and emotional intelligence. One or the other alone will not suffice. Only by mastering both will the leader succeed. For example, former president William Clinton was rendered ineffective as a leader because of the Monica Lewinsky affair and was almost impeached. Why? Because he suddenly lost the *knowledge* of how government works (science)? No! He lost his ability to lead because he lost the *trust and respect* of much of the American public (art). He could still lead with his mind, but he had lost the ability to lead with his heart.

On the other hand, one could argue that former president Jimmie Carter lost his ability to lead because of a perceived lack of competency. The majority of the voting public did not believe that he had the knowledge necessary to manage government operations and effectively lead with mind. However, virtually no one questioned his concern for people and his ability to lead with heart. Absent the perceived ability to do *both*, however, he lost the 1980 election to Ronald Reagan.

I conclude, then, that effective leaders are situational; that is, they are capable of adapting their leadership behavior to the situation. They utilize structural, human resource, symbolic, and political leadership behavior when appropriate. They lead with both mind (structural and political behavior) and with heart (human resource and symbolic behavior). They master both the science (mind) and art (heart) of leadership, and in doing so, they are transformational, leading their organizations to new heights. As Chris Lowney writes in *Heroic Leadership*, such leaders are, in a word, truly "heroic."

ORGANIZATIONAL CULTURE

Effectively balancing the use of the four frames of leadership behavior assumes that the leader has a thorough knowledge and understanding of his or her organizational culture. In the words of Harold Hill in *The Music Man*, the leader needs "to know the territory." Knowing the territory, or knowing the organizational culture, means that the leader must know the beliefs, expectations, and shared values of the organization, as well as the personality of the individuals and the organization as a whole. Without such knowledge, the leader cannot appropriately apply the correct leadership frame behavior to a given situation.

As mentioned in chapter 1, Paul Hersey and Ken Blanchard contribute to our understanding of what it means to know the culture of the organization with their concept of the *readiness level*. They define readiness level as the follower's ability and willingness to accomplish a specific task; this is the major contingency that influences what leadership frame behavior should be applied. Follower readiness incorporates the follower's level of achievement, motivation, ability, and willingness to assume responsibility for his or her own behavior in accomplishing specific tasks, as well as his or her education and experience relevant to the task. So, a person with a low readiness level should be dealt with by using structural frame behavior (telling behavior), while a person with a very high readiness level should be dealt with using human resource and symbolic frame behavior (delegating behavior).

At this point, the reader may be thinking that using leadership theory to determine one's leadership behavior is an exercise in futility. How can one realistically be expected to assess accurately and immediately the individual's or group's readiness level before acting. It seems like an utterly complex and overwhelming task. When confronted with this reaction, I relate using leadership theory to determine one's leadership behavior to riding a bike. When we first learn to ride a bike, we have to concern ourselves with keeping our balance, steering, pedaling, and being ready to brake at a moment's notice. However, once we have experience riding the bike, we seldom think of those details. We have learned to ride the bike by instinct or habit. Having used situational leadership theory to determine my own leadership behavior, I can attest to the fact that its use becomes as instinctive as riding a bike after awhile. At this point, I can almost always instantly assess the readiness level of an individual or group and apply the appropriate leadership frame behavior—and believe me when I tell you that if I can do it, so can you.

TRANSFORMATIONAL LEADERSHIP

We all aspire to be transformational leaders—leaders who inspire positive change in their followers. As we saw in chapter 1, charismatic or transformational leaders use charisma to inspire their followers. They talk to their followers about how essential their performance is and how they expect the group's performance to exceed expectations. Such leaders use dominance, self-confidence, a need for influence, and conviction of moral righteousness to increase their charisma and, consequently, their leadership effectiveness. A transformational leader changes an organization by recognizing an opportunity and developing a vision, communicating that vision to organizational members, building trust in the vision, and achieving the vision by motivating organizational members.

Virtually all of the coaches profiled in this book could be considered transformational leaders. In almost every case, they moved their organizations from being ineffective to being extremely effective. Most of them inherited losing teams, only to transform them not only into winning programs but into supremely effective ones—they all won either a national championship or a Super Bowl. They achieved this success by displaying the characteristics of a transformational leader. They all had a vision and the personal charisma and ability to convince others to join them in achieving that vision. However, they did so in different ways by applying the appropriate leadership behavior to their differing situations. They were able to gauge the *readiness level* of their followers accurately and apply the appropriate leadership behavior, be it structural, human resource, symbolic, or political frame behavior, or some combination thereof. Although this is easier said than done, studying these coaches' leadership behavior as depicted in this book should be helpful to anyone aspiring to become a transformational leader.

CONCLUSION

Recently, a plethora of research studies have been conducted on leadership and leadership styles. The overwhelming evidence indicates that there is no one singular leadership style that is most effective in all situations. Rather, it has been found that a leader's leadership behavior should be adapted to the situation so that, at various times, structural, human resource, symbolic, or political frame leadership behavior may be most effective.

The emergence of transformational leadership has seen leadership theory come full circle. Transformational leadership theory combines aspects of early trait theory with the more current situational models. The personal charisma of the leader, along with his or her ability to formulate an organizational vision and communicate it to others, determines the transformational leader's effectiveness.

Since the effective leader is expected to adapt his or her leadership style to an ever-changing environment, leadership becomes an even more complex and challenging task. However, a thorough knowledge of one's organizational culture and of leadership theory can make some sense of the apparent chaos that a leader faces on a daily basis. It is my hope that this text will shed some light on the *situation*.

REFERENCES

Biggart, N. W. & Hamilton, G. G. (1987). An institutional theory of leadership, *Journal of Applied Behavioral Sciences* 234: 429–441.

Bolman, Lee B. & Deal, Terrance E. (1991). *Reframing Organizations: Artistry, Choice, and Leadership*. San Francisco, Jossey-Bass.

Bowden, B. (2001). *The Bowden Way: 50 Years of Leadership Wisdom*. Atlanta: Longstreet Press.

Bryant, P., & Underwood, J. (1974). *Bear: My Life and Good Times as Alabama's Head Coach*. Boston: Little, Brown & Company.

Chapple, Christopher (1993). *The Jesuit Tradition in Education and Missions*. Scranton: University of Scranton Press.

Conger, A. & Kanungo, R. N. (1987). Toward a behavioral theory of charismatic leadership in organizational settings, *Academy of Management Review* 12: 637–647.

DePree, Max (1989). *Leadership is an Art*. New York, Dell Publishing.

Documents of the 34th Generel Congregation of the Society of Jesus (1995). St. Louis: The Institute of Jesuit Sources.

Dungy, T. (2007). *Quiet Strength: The Principles, Practices and Priorities of a Winning Life*. Illinois: Tyndale House.

Erickson, F. (1984). School Literacy, Reasoning and Civility: An Anthropologist's Perspective, *Review of Educational Research* 54: 525–546.

Fiedler, F. E. & Chemers, M. M. (1984). *Improving Leadership Effectiveness: The Leader Match Concept*, 2nd ed. New York: Wiley.

Fiedler , F. E. & Garcia, J. E. (1987). *New Approaches to Effective Leadership.* New York: Wiley.

Field, R. H. G. (1982). A test of the Vroom-Yetton normative model of leadership, *Journal of Applied Psychology* 67: 523–532.

Fleishman, E. & Harris, E. (1959). Patterns of leadership behavior related to employee grievances and turnover, *Personnel Psychology* 1: 45–53.

Fleishman, E., Harris, E. F., & Buret, R. D. (1955). *Leadership and Supervision in Industry.* Columbus: Ohio State University Press.

Foster, William (1986). *Paradigms and Promises.* New York: Prometheus Books.

Gibbs, J., & Jenkins, J. (1991). *Joe Gibbs: Fourth and One.* Nashville: Thomas Nelson Publishers.

Gibbs, J., & Abraham, K. (2003). *Racing to Win.* Sisters, Oregon: Multnomah Publishers.

Glasser, William (1984). *Control Theory: A New Explanation of How We Control Our Lives.* New York, Harper and Row.

Griffiths, D. & Ribbins, Peter (1995). *Leadership Matters in Education: Regarding Secondary Headship.* Inaugural Lecture, University of Birmingham, Edgbaston.

Gutman, B. (2000). *Parcells: A Biography.* New York: Carroll & Graf Publishers.

Halberstam, D. (2005). *The Education of a Coach.* New York: Hyperion Books.

Hersey, P. & Blanchard, K. H. (1998) *Management of Organizational Behavior,* 5th ed. Englewood Cliffs, N.J.: Prentice-Hall.

Holley, M. (2004). *Patriot Reign: Bill Belechick, the Coaches and Players Who Built a Champion.* New York: Harper Collins Publishers.

House, R. J. (1971). A path-goal theory of leader effectiveness, *Administrative Science Quarterly* 16: 321–338.

House, R. J. (1997). A 1976 theory of charismatic leadership. In J. G. Hunt and Larson, eds., *Leadership: The Cutting Edge.* Carbondale, IL: Southern Illinois University Press.

House, R. J. & Mitchell, T. R. (1974). Path-goal theory of leadership, *Journal of Contemporary Business* (Autumn): 81–97.

Johnson, J., & Hinton, E. (1993). *Turning the Thing Around: Pulling America's Team Out of the Dumps and Myself Out of the Doghouse.* New York: Hyperion Books.

Kirkpatrick S. A. & Locke, E. A. (1991). Leadership: Do traits matter? *Academy of Management Executive* 5(2): 49.

La Monte, B., & Shook, R. (2004). *Winning the NFL Way: Leadership Lessons from Football's Top Head Coaches.* New York: Harper Collins Publishers.

McGregor, D. (1961). *The Human Side of Enterprise.* New York: McGraw-Hill.

REFERENCES

REFERENCES

Mintzberg, H. (1979.) *The Nature of Managerial Work*, 2nd ed. Englewood Cliffs, N.J.: Prentice-Hall.

Pagna, T., & Parseghian, A. (1976). *Notre Dames's Era of Ara.* Huntsville, Alabama: The Strode Publishers.

Parcells, B. (1987). *Parcells: Autobiography of the Biggest Giant of Them All.* New York: Bonus Books.

Parcells, B., & Coplon, J. (1995). *Finding a Way to Win: The Principles of Leadership, Teamwork and Motivation.* New York: Doubleday.

Paterno, J. (1959). *Paterno: By the Book.* New York: Random House.

Paterno, J. (2007). *We are Penn State.* New York: Mascot Books.

Paterno, J. & Asbell, B. (1989). *Paterno: By the Book.* New York: Berkley Publications.

Ravier, Andre, SJ. (1987). *Ignatius of Loyola and the Founding of the Society of Jesus.* San Francisco: Ignatius Press.

Schein, E. H. (1974). The Hawthorne Studies Revisited: A defense of Theory Y. Sloan School of Management Working Paper #756-74. Cambridge: Massachusetts Institute of Technology, p. 3.

Senge, Peter M. (1990). *The Fifth Dimension: The Art of Practice of the Learning Organization.* New York, Doubleday.

Shula, D., & Blanchard, K. (1995). *Everyone's A Coach.* New York: Harper Business.

Solzhenitsyn, A. (1978). *A World Split Apart.* New York: Harper and Row, pp. 17–19.

Stogdill, R. M. & Coons, A. E., eds. (1957). *Leader Behavior: Its Description and Measurement.* Columbus: Ohio State University Bureau of Business Research.

Toner, Jules J., SJ (1991). *Discerning God's Will: Ignatius of Loyola's Teaching on Christian Decision Making.* St. Louis: The Institute of Jesuit Sources.

Tripole, Martin R., SJ (1994). *Faith Beyond Justice.* St. Louis: The Institute of Jesuit Sources.

Vroom, V. H. & Jago, A. G. (1988). *The New Leadership: Managing Participation in Organizations.* Englewood Cliffs, N.J.: Prentice-Hall.

Vroom, V. H. & Yetton, P. W. (1973). *Leadership and Decision Making.* Pittsburgh: University of Pittsburgh Press.

Walsh, B. (1990). *Building a Champion: On Football and the Making of the 49ers.* New York: St. Martin's Press.

Walsh, B., & Dickey, G. (1998). *Bill Walsh: Finding the Winning Edge.* Champaign, Illinois: Sports Publishing Inc.

Wikipedia.org.

Willner, A. R. (1984). *The Spellbinders: Charismatic Political Leadership.* New Haven, Conn.: Yale University Press.

APPENDIX: THE HEART SMART ORGANIZATIONAL DIAGNOSIS MODEL

Just as there are vital signs in measuring individual health, I believe that there are vital signs in measuring the health of organizations. This survey will help identify those vital signs in your school system. The purpose of the Heart Smart Organizational Diagnosis Questionnaire, therefore, is to provide feedback data for intensive diagnostic efforts. Use of the questionnaire, either by itself or in conjunction with other information-collecting techniques such as systematic observation or interviewing, will provide the data needed for identifying strengths and weaknesses in the functioning of an educational institution and help determine whether the leaders are leading with both mind and heart.

A meaningful diagnostic effort must be based on a theory or model of organizational development. This makes action research possible, as it facilitates problem identification, which is essential to determining the proper functioning of an organization. The model suggested here establishes a systematic approach for analyzing relationships among the variables that influence how an organization is managed. It provides information for assessment of ten areas of formal and informal activity: structure, identity and culture, leadership, motivation, communication, decision making, conflict resolution, goal setting and planning, power distribution, and attitude toward change. The outer circle in Figure A.1 is an organizational boundary for diagnosis. This

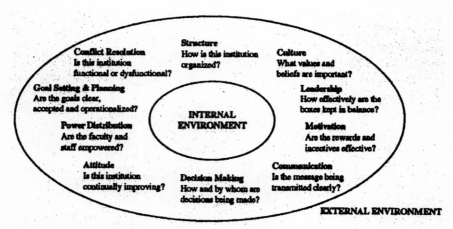

Figure A.I.   Organizational boundaries for analysis.

boundary demarcates the functioning of the internal and external environments. Since the underlying organizational theory upon which this survey is based is an open systems model, it is essential that influences from both the internal and external environment be considered for the analysis to be complete.

Please think of your *present personal or professional environment* and indicate the degree to which you agree or disagree with each of the following statements. A "1" is *Disagree* Strongly and a "7" is *Agree* Strongly.

Disagree Strongly	Disagree	Disagree Slightly	Neither Agree Nor Disagree	Agree Slightly	Agree	Agree Strongly
1	2	3	4	5	6	7

1. The manner in which the tasks in this institution are divided is logical.
2. The relationships among co-workers are harmonious.
3. This institution's leadership efforts result in the fulfillment of its purposes.
4. My work at this institution offers me an opportunity to grow as a person.

5. I can always talk to someone at work, if I have a work-related problem.
6. The faculty actively participates in decisions.
7. There is little evidence of unresolved conflict in this institution.
8. There is a strong fit between this institution's mission and my own values.
9. The faculty and staff are represented on most committees and task forces.
10. Staff development routinely accompanies any significant changes that occur in this institution.
11. The manner in which the tasks in this institution are distributed is fair.
12. Older faculty's opinions are valued.
13. The administrators display the behaviors required for effective leadership.
14. The rewards and incentives here are both internal and external.
15. There is open and direct communication among all levels of this institution.
16. Participative decision making is fostered at this institution.
17. What little conflict exists at this institution is not dysfunctional.
18. Representatives of all segments of the school community participate in the strategic planning process.
19. The faculty and staff have an appropriate voice in the operation of this institution.
20. This institution is not resistant to constructive change.
21. The division of labor in this organization helps its efforts to reach its goals.
22. I feel valued by this institution.
23. The administration encourages an appropriate amount of participation in decision making.
24. Faculty and staff members are often recognized for special achievements.
25. There are no significant barriers to effective communication at this institution.

26. When the acceptance of a decision is important, a group decision-making model is used.
27. Mechanisms at this institution effectively manage conflict and stress.
28. Most of the employees understand the mission and goals of this institution.
29. The faculty and staff feel empowered to make their own decisions regarding their daily work.
30. Tolerance toward change is modeled by the administration of this institution.
31. The various grade-level teachers and departments work well together.
32. Differences among people are accepted.
33. The leadership is able to generate continuous improvement in the institution.
34. My ideas are encouraged, recognized, and used.
35. Communication is carried out in a non-aggressive style.
36. In general, the decision-making process is effective.
37. Conflicts are usually resolved before they become dysfunctional.
38. For the most part, the employees of this institution feel an "ownership" of its goals.
39. The faculty and staff are encouraged to be creative in their work.
40. When changes are made, they do so within a rational process.
41. This institution's organizational design responds well to changes in the internal and external environment.
42. The teaching and the non-teaching staffs get along with one another.
43. The leadership of this institution espouses a clear educational vision.
44. The goals and objectives for the year are mutually developed by the faculty and the administration.
45. I believe that my opinions and ideas are listened to.
46. Usually, a collaborative style of decision making is utilized at this institution.

47. A collaborative approach to conflict resolution is ordinarily used.
48. This institution has a clear educational vision.
49. The faculty and staff can express their opinions without fear of retribution.
50. I feel confident that I will have an opportunity for input if a significant change were to take place in this institution.
51. This institution is "people-oriented."
52. Administrators and faculty have mutual respect for one another.
53. Administrators give people the freedom to do their job.
54. The rewards and incentives in this institution are designed to satisfy a variety of individual needs.
55. The opportunity for feedback is always available in the communications process.
56. Group decision-making techniques, like brainstorming and group surveys, are sometimes used in the decision-making process.
57. Conflicts are often prevented by early intervention.
58. This institution has a strategic plan for the future.
59. Most administrators here use the power of persuasion rather than the power of coercion.
60. This institution is committed to continually improving through the process of change.
61. This institution does not adhere to a strict chain of command.
62. This institution exhibits grace, style, and civility.
63. The administrators model desired behavior.
64. At this institution, employees are not normally coerced into doing things.
65. I have the information that I need to do a good job.
66. I can constructively challenge the decisions in this institution.
67. A process to resolve work-related grievances is available.
68. This institution has an ongoing planning process.
69. The faculty and staff have input into the operation of this institution through a collective bargaining unit or through a faculty governance body.
70. The policies, procedures, and programs of this institution are periodically reviewed.

HEART SMART SCORING SHEET

Instructions: Transfer the numbers you circled on the questionnaire to the blanks below. Add each column and divide each sum by seven. This will give you comparable scores for each of the ten areas.

Structure	*Identity and Culture*	*Leadership*	*Motivation*
1 _____	2 _____	3 _____	4 _____
11 _____	12 _____	13 _____	14 _____
21 _____	22 _____	23 _____	24 _____
31 _____	32 _____	33 _____	34 _____
41 _____	42 _____	43 _____	44 _____
51 _____	52 _____	53 _____	54 _____
61 _____	62 _____	63 _____	64 _____

Total

_____   _____   _____   _____

Average

_____   _____   _____   _____

Communication	*Decision Making*	*Conflict Resolution*	*Goal Setting/ Planning*
5 _____	6 _____	7 _____	8 _____
15 _____	16 _____	17 _____	18 _____
25 _____	26 _____	27 _____	28 _____
35 _____	36 _____	37 _____	38 _____
45 _____	46 _____	47 _____	48 _____
55 _____	56 _____	57 _____	58 _____
65 _____	66 _____	67 _____	68 _____

Total

_____   _____   _____   _____

Average

_____   _____   _____   _____

Power Distribution	*Attitude Toward Change*
9 _____	10 _____
19 _____	20 _____
29 _____	30 _____
39 _____	40 _____
49 _____	50 _____
59 _____	60 _____
69 _____	70 _____

Total

_____   _____

Average

_____   _____

INTERPRETATION SHEET

Instructions: Study the background information and interpretation suggestions that follow.

Background

The Heart Smart Organizational Diagnosis Questionnaire is a survey-feedback instrument designed to collect data on organizational functioning. It measures the perceptions of persons in an organization to determine areas of activity that would benefit from an organizational development effort. It can be used as the sole data-collection technique or in conjunction with other techniques (interview, observation, etc.). The instrument and the model reflect a systematic approach for analyzing relationships among variables that influence how an organization is managed. Using the Heart Smart Organizational Diagnosis Questionnaire is the first step in determining appropriate interventions for organizational change efforts.

Interpretation and Diagnosis

A crucial consideration is the diagnosis based on data interpretation. The simplest diagnosis would be to assess the amount of variance for each of the ten variables in relation to a score of 4, which is the neutral point. Scores below 4 would indicate a problem with organizational functioning. The closer the score is to 1, the more severe the problem would be. Scores above 4 indicate the lack of a problem, with a score of 7 indicating optimum functioning.

Another diagnostic approach follows the same guidelines of assessment in relation to the neutral point (score) of 4. The score of each of the 70 items on the questionnaire can be reviewed to produce more exacting information on problematic areas. Thus, diagnosis would be more precise. For example, let us suppose that the average score on item number 8 is 1.4. This would indicate not only a problem in organizational purpose or goal setting, but also a more specific problem in that there is a gap between organizational and individual goals. This more precise diagnostic effort is likely to lead to a more appropriate intervention in the organization than the generalized diagnostic approach described in the preceding paragraph.

Appropriate diagnosis must address the relationships between the boxes to determine the interconnectedness of problems. For example, if there is a problem with *communication*, it could be that the organizational *structure* does not foster effective communication. This might be the case if the average score on item 25 was well below 4 (2.5 or lower) and all the items on organizational *structure* (1, 11, 21, 31, 41, 51, 61) averaged below 4.

Breinigsville, PA USA
22 April 2010
236570BV00003B/1/P